MORE SWAMP COOKIN'

ANOTHER BATCH OF RECIPES FROM
THE LOUISIANA BAYOU

MORE SWAMP COOKIN'

ANOTHER BATCH OF RECIPES FROM THE LOUISIANA BAYOU

DANA HOLYFIELD

TEN SPEED PRESS
BERKELEY TORONTO

Ten Speed Press
P.O. Box 7123
Berkeley, California 94707
www.tenspeed.com

Distributed in Australia by Simon and Schuster Australia, in Canada by Ten Speed Press Canada, in New Zealand by Southern Publishers Group, in South Africa by Real Books, in Southeast Asia by Berkeley Books, and in the United Kingdom and Europe by Airlift Books.

Book design by Victor Mingovits, NYC
All photos copyright © 2001 by Dana Holyfield
Library of Congress Cataloging-in-Publication Data on file with the publisher.

First printing, 2001
Printed in Canada

1 2 3 4 5 6 7 8 9 10 — 05 04 03 02 01

CONTENTS

CHAPTER 4
LIFE ON THE RIVER: STICK TO THE RIBS SOUPS AND STEWS **85**

CHAPTER 5
THE SPICE OF LIFE: SIDE DISHES AND DESSERTS..............**105**

CHAPTER 6
THE LOWDOWN ON GATOR AND LOUANN: GET-TOGETHER FOODS **131**

INTRODUCTION

Before the Gator Bandit lets the gator loose, I'd like to express my deep appreciation to all the folks in the Honey Island Swamp. I know how they pretty much like to keep to themselves, except on Saturday nights, and some of them don't really like the idea of being famous, especially if it has anything to do with a jail sentence. But, they said they reckon this kind of exposure wouldn't hurt none, as long as we didn't use their real names unless I got their consent. If you read my first *Swamp Cookin'*, then you will be familiar with some of the folks in this book. If you didn't get to read it yet, get a hold of yourself because you're in for a heck of a good time. This is the kind of lifestyle heard about only through the Muskydine Vine. At the Saturday gatherings at the camps and houseboats along the Pearl River, I was able to round up some more tall tales and short tales about swamp outlaws and in-laws, good times and bad times. I gathered more tasty swamp recipes recited by the River People and was allowed to make a resourceful collection of new pictures so outsiders can see for themselves how we do the Swamp Woogie Boogie.

THE SWAMP GROCERY LIST

A couple of 4-foot gators

Catfish and white perch

Couple of sacks of crawfish

A few big turtles

One or two nutria

Deer and wild hog

THE RIVER PEOPLE'S FREEZER STORAGE FOR OFF MONTHS

Deer steak and deer sausage

Wild boar sausage

Catfish and gar

Wood ducks, rabbit, squirrels

Plenty of bags of ice

THE SWAMP WOOGIE BOOGIE

The Swamp Woogie Boogie is something to do with kicking your heels up on the dance floor, messing around the Mayhal tree, meddling in Nana's kitchen, hunting in the holler, snaking around the cypress tree, shooting the bullfrog, and whatnot. I suppose it means whatever you want it to mean in the Louisiana Swamps.

ORDERING AND SHIPPING FOOD FROM THE SWAMP

To have alligator, blue crab, crabmeat, crawfish, frog legs, oysters, shrimp, soft-shell crab, turtle, cajun sausage, gumbo, and more delivered fresh to your door overnight anywhere in the country, contact New Orleans Over Night, Inc. (800) NU-AWLINS; www.nuawlins.com.

INGREDIENTS IN THE CAMP PANTRY

Tony Chachere's Creole and Cajun Seasonings

Cayenne pepper, black pepper, and salt

Couple of big jars of crab boil

Bottle of Worcestershire sauce

Couple of boxes of fish fry

Flour and cornmeal

Couple of gallons of cooking oil

Big sack of potatoes and onions

Ketchup

Big can of community coffee

Jar of dry dairy creamer and sugar

Can of corned beef for emergencies

～ STUFF ～ YOU MIGHT FIND IN THE CAMP ICEBOX

Left-over deer roast or deer
  meat chili

Deer sausage

Horseradish and tartar sauce

Jug of drinking water

1/2 gallon of milk

Bottle of wine

A cold beer somebody
  overlooked

CHAPTER 1

MORNING ON THE RIVER: BREAKFAST IN CAMP

 SWAMP FESTIVITY

On a typical Louisiana Saturday night at the river camps and houseboats in the swamp, some of the folks go grocery shopping at the swamp market. They pick up a few things for supper, or should I say they catch a few things, or shoot them. Whichever is more appropriate at the time. When they return to the camp, they target somebody who hasn't done much that day, except shoot the bull. They ask them to skin dinner. Somebody else who can cook pretty good gets volunteered to whip up something tasty to eat. After everybody's devoured the savory swamp cuisine that you won't hardly find on a menu anywhere else in the world, they can shake a leg, hoot and holler and drink 'til they are fit to be tied. When morning rolls around, they talk all about it while eating leftovers from the night before, or making camp-style beignets and drinking a strong cup of spoon-in-the-mud Louisiana-style Cafe A'lai to help cure their suffering.

CURE FOR THE COMMON HANGOVER

Coffee with chicory will get your blood pumping. The best kind to do the job is Community Coffee or CDM, both made right here in Louisiana. Or some folks at the camp choose to drink another cold beer overlooked in somebody's ice chest.

If someone is up and stirring after one of those strong cups of Camp Cafe A'lai, they get sent on a boat ride and a truck ride to the EZ Serve up the road to get a few snacks to hold them over until someone checks the fish traps, or shows up with gator meat or a fresh sack of crawfish. No matter how much food is left over from the night before, a whole new day calls for a whole new meal fresh out the holler.

CAMP-STYLE BEIGNETS

2 cups of vegetable oil

2 cans of refrigerator-style biscuit dough

1 (8-ounce) box of confectioners' sugar for coating

Heat oil in heavy saucepan or deep fryer to 375°. Roll biscuit dough into beignets, 1/4 inch thick; seal edges of dough by pinching with fingers. Drop beignets, one at a time, into hot oil. Fry beignets until golden brown on both sides, turning once. Scoop browned beignets from oil using a slotted spoon and drain on paper towels.

Pour confectioners' sugar into a paper sack. Add warm beignets, several at a time, and shake to coat thoroughly. Serve with Cafe A'lai.

MOM'S SOUTHERN CORNBREAD

1/4 inch vegetable oil for frying

1 cup self-rising cornmeal

1 tablespoon sugar

3/4 cup milk

1 egg

Mom says a large cast-iron skillet is a must. Heat skillet until oil is hot. Sprinkle with a little cornmeal. In a separate bowl, mix batter of cornmeal, sugar, milk, and egg. Mix well and pour into hot skillet. Bake 40 minutes at 375°, until cornbread is golden brown. Remove from oven and butter while hot.

GRANDMA EMILY'S BUTTERMILK BISCUITS

2 tablespoons sugar

1 cup Crisco

2 cups self-rising flour

1 cup buttermilk

In old Tupelo Gum Mixing Bowl (or some other kind of large mixing bowl), cream together sugar and shortening, then cut in flour with a fork until the mixture is crumbly. Add buttermilk and knead until dough is pliable. Roll out dough 1/2 inch thick with rolling pin. Cut biscuits with a fruit jar or biscuit cutter. Bake on greased baking sheet at 350° until light brown.

UNCLE DALE'S CAMP BREAD

2 cups flour

1 cup Crisco

1 cup water

3 tablespoons sugar

IMPORTANT: You must use a cast-iron skillet to make this so it will taste good. Mix ingredients together in a bowl. Add mixture to greased cast-iron skillet. Cover and cook on medium heat on stove burner. Cook 45 minutes, or until bread is done and browned on top.

CRAWFISH OMELETTE

1 pound crawfish tails, peeled

1/2 cup (1 stick) butter

1/2 cup chopped green onions

1 clove garlic, minced

1/2 cup chopped parsley

8 eggs

Salt and pepper

1/2 teaspoon Worcestershire sauce

1/2 teaspoon Tony Chachere's Creole Seasoning

Sauté crawfish tails in butter over low heat for 10 minutes. Add green onions, garlic, and parsley. In a large bowl, beat eggs with salt, pepper, Worcestershire sauce, and Tony Chachere's. Add eggs to crawfish and cook until eggs are firm.

GRANDMA JEANETTE'S EGGS GOLDEN ROD

6 hard-boiled eggs

Salt and pepper

1 pack sausage patties

Flour

1 loaf of bread, toasted

Peel eggs. Use a fork to mash them finely, then season with salt and pepper. In a large skillet, brown sausage. Remove sausage but save grease in pan to make roux with flour.

Sprinkle a spoonful of smashed eggs on top of each slice of toasted bread. Pour the roux on top of eggs. Serve sausage on side, or crumble the sausage into the roux and serve on top of the eggs and toast.

UNCLE DALE'S ANGELINE BREAKFAST SANDWICH

2 cups instant biscuit mix

1 cup milk

2 eggs

Salt and pepper

Bacon

Syrup

To make this recipe, you will need to cook the pancakes, eggs, and bacon in three different skillets.

In a mixing bowl, prepare pancake batter by combining biscuit mix and milk. Cook pancakes in skillet following biscuit mix package directions.

In a separate bowl, beat eggs. Pour into a skillet or omelette pan and cook over medium-low heat. Cook eggs flat; don't stir or scramble them. Season with salt and pepper.

In another skillet, fry bacon.

Layer cooked eggs and bacon on top of each pancake; squirt syrup over it, then fold the pancake and serve.

GRANDDADDY'S BEER BISCUITS

1 bottle of beer

3 cups instant biscuit mix

2 tablespoons sugar

In a mixing bowl, stir beer into biscuit mix and add sugar. Drop spoonfuls onto well-greased baking sheets. Bake at 375° until brown.

CHAPTER 2

GONE FISHIN': FISH AND SHELLFISH

 **THE YOUNG AND THE ROWDY**

Jimmy Joe's boys were in real big trouble when they got into Old Man Chester's stash of moonshine that he kept hidden in his boat. Old Man Chester had passed out right at dark like he always does, so Billy Bob and Tommy Joe snuck into his boat and swiped the milk jug with the word "poison" written on it. They gathered their buddies over at Cousin Leroy's houseboat and drank that moonshine 'til they were plum crazy.

Before they got sick and passed out, they decided to run Old Man Chester's trotlines. After checking each hook and taking off all the fish and turtles and eels, they forgot to rebait the lines. When they got back to the houseboat, nobody felt like skinning and cleaning the fish, so they threw them back into the river.

When Old Man Chester woke up at midnight, which is usually the time he wakes up to check his lines, he just couldn't understand why in the world there wasn't one fish or turtle on any of his hooks. Being a superstitious fool, Old Man Chester thought it was a bad sign and he rushed over to his cousin's camp downriver to warn everybody to take cover.

That's when someone ratted out Jimmy Joe's boys being sprawled out in the middle of Leroy's houseboat with one of Old

Man Chester's empty milk jugs and a full bucket of shiners. Old Man Chester snatched up his boat paddle and whacked them boys 'til they woke up and he made them walk the line—trotline that is—for the rest of their summer vacation.

Jimmy Joe asked his boys if they learned their lesson and the oldest boy said, "Yes, sir, we'll never throw the fish back again."

LOUISIANA REDFISH COURT BOUILLON

1 cup flour

3/4 cup oil

1 bell pepper, finely chopped

1 cup finely chopped onion

1 (14-ounce) can stewed tomatoes

2 (8-ounce) cans tomato paste

3 cloves garlic, minced

1 cup chopped celery

1 lemon, thinly sliced

2 bay leaves

Salt and pepper

4 cups hot water

4 pounds redfish, deboned
(leave skin on for better flavor)

1 tablespoon parsley, finely chopped

1 tablespoon Worcestershire sauce

2 cups sauterne wine

2 (4-ounce) cans chopped mushrooms

1/2 cup chopped green or black olives

In a heavy skillet, make a dark roux with flour and oil. Add bell pepper and onion. Stir and cook until vegetables are well smothered. Add stewed tomatoes and tomato paste. Cook thoroughly. Add garlic, celery, lemon slices, and bay leaves. Season with salt and pepper. Add hot water, a little at a time, up to 4 cups. Simmer 15 minutes. Add redfish. Bring to a boil and cook 30 minutes. Add parsley, Worcestershire sauce, wine, mushrooms, and olives. Bring to a boil and cook 5 minutes. Turn off heat and let stand, covered, for a few minutes. Serve with rice on the side or with bread.

GASPERGOU SAUCE PICANTE

NOTE: If gaspergou is unavailable,
substitute catfish, redfish, or trout.

5 pounds gaspergou

2 cups chopped onion

1/2 cup vegetable oil

1 cup chopped celery

2 cloves garlic, minced

1 bell pepper, chopped

1 (8-ounce) can tomato paste

1 (4-ounce) can tomato sauce

Juice and rind of 1 lemon

Salt to taste

Cayenne pepper to taste

1/4 cup chopped green onions

1/4 cup chopped parsley

In a large pot, boil fish with just enough water to
cover, long enough to debone easily. Keep fish
stock for later.

In a heavy skillet, sauté onions in oil until transparent. Add celery, garlic, bell pepper, tomato paste, tomato sauce, lemon rind, salt, and cayenne pepper. Cook 40 minutes on low heat.

Add 1½ cups fish stock. Add lemon juice, green onions, and parsley. Add gaspergou to sauce and simmer for 20 minutes. Serve over white rice.

BIG EASY SHRIMP AND OKRA GUMBO

1 quart chopped okra

1 onion, chopped

1 bell pepper, chopped

3 tomatoes, peeled and chopped

1 tablespoon vegetable oil

1 teaspoon salt

1/2 teaspoon black pepper

2 cups shrimp, peeled and cleaned

1 quart water

In a skillet, sauté okra with onion, bell pepper, and tomatoes in oil for 15 minutes. Add salt, pepper, shrimp, and water. Cook on low heat for 45 minutes. Serve with white rice.

PAP'S TROUT PUPPIES

1 pound trout fillets

1 teaspoon salt

Peanut oil for deep frying

4 tablespoons baking powder

2 cups self-rising flour

3 cups cornmeal

1 large yellow onion, chopped

1/2 cup sugar

1 (14-ounce) can of whole kernel corn, drained

Salt and pepper

Boil fillets in water with 1 teaspoon salt. While trout is boiling, heat oil in deep-fat fryer to 375°.

In a large mixing bowl, combine the trout with the remaining ingredients, mixing well.

Use a wet teaspoon to scoop out mixture and drop in hot oil. Dip the teaspoon in water between scoops of batter. Cook each trout and corn puppy until it floats and turns golden brown. Remove and cool on paper towels. Serve with ketchup.

UNCLE PERRY'S TUNA PUPPIES

2 (12-ounce) cans tuna

1 (14-ounce) can asparagus tips, chopped

1 onion, chopped

1 bunch green onions, finely chopped

2 cloves garlic, finely chopped

1 1/2 cups cornmeal

1/2 cup flour

2 eggs

1/2 cup milk

1 teaspoon salt

1/2 teaspoon pepper

Dash of Tony Chachere's Cajun Seasoning

Vegetable oil for deep frying

In a mixing bowl, beat together all ingredients. Mixture should be stiff enough to drop by spoonfuls into hot oil. Deep fry until tuna puppies float and turn golden brown on both sides. Remove and drain on paper towels.

VIOLA'S CRAB PUPPIES

1 cup crabmeat, cut into small chunks

1 cup cornmeal

1/2 cup flour

3/4 cup cream corn

1/4 cup chopped green onions

Salt and pepper

1 tablespoon Creole seasoning

Vegetable oil for frying

In a large bowl, combine all ingredients except oil until well mixed.

Heat oil in a large, heavy frying pan. Dip a teaspoon in water and scoop up a heaping teaspoon of batter; drop it in the hot oil. Turn the crab puppy until both sides are golden brown. Do not overcook. Dip the teaspoon in water between each scoop of batter. Remove the cooked crab puppies and place on paper towels to drain.

BAKED LEMON-GARLIC OYSTERS

2 dozen raw oysters

Juice of 1 large lemon

Garlic salt

Lemon pepper seasoning mix

2 cloves garlic, minced

1/2 cup butter

Butter a 9-by-13-inch baking pan. Place oysters in the pan. Squeeze lemon juice all over oysters. Sprinkle with garlic salt, lemon pepper seasoning, and minced garlic. Dot chunks of butter around oysters. Bake at 350° for 15 to 20 minutes.

CREAMED OYSTER PASTA

1 (1-pound) package pasta

1/2 cup butter

1 (8-ounce) package cream cheese

1 bunch green onions, chopped

3 cloves garlic, chopped

2 dozen raw oysters

1/2 cup milk

Salt and pepper

Prepare pasta according to package instructions. You can use whatever type of pasta you like—rotini, shells, spaghetti.

In a large saucepan, melt butter and cream cheese. Add green onions and garlic, then oysters, milk, salt, and pepper. Stir on medium heat until oysters begin to curl, about 10 minutes. Reduce heat and add cooked pasta to creamed oyster sauce. Serve.

VERN'S CREAM SHRIMP SPAGHETTI

1 pound spaghetti

1 onion, chopped

1 bell pepper, chopped

2 stalks celery, chopped

Olive oil

Salt and pepper

Garlic salt

1 pound shrimp, deveined and peeled

16 ounces sour cream

In a large saucepan, boil spaghetti according to the package instructions. In a separate skillet, sauté onion, bell pepper, and celery in olive oil. Season to taste with salt, pepper, and garlic salt. Add shrimp and cook until pink. Turn off heat and stir in sour cream. Add cooked and drained spaghetti, mix well, and serve.

❧ THE OLD AND SHORT-FUSED ❧

Old Man Stan was minding his own beeswax at his houseboat when some Mississippi boys moved into his slough around the bend. He didn't like the idea of having close neighbors from out of town, but when they started calling on his fish with a telephone doohickey invented by a fish bandit, that just did it.

Old Man Stan wasn't in a suitable mood that day to start with because the Mississippi boys had made him seasick when they sped by in their boat that had an Iroc Z engine, ignoring his "No Wake" sign. He had been planning to sleep in that day after his long night out frogging.

Old Man Stan decided to have his bath in the river. While scrubbing the mud from between his toes, he noticed a mess of fish popping up to the surface. He decided he's had enough of that commotion. The Mississippi boys had passed the limit. So he climbed back into his houseboat, slipped into his camouflage gear, got his buckshot and waited 'til they passed by.

When they did, he fired a round of buckshot above them and told them to stick up their hands (he didn't want to wound them just yet). Knowing Old Man Stan's reputation, the Mississippi boys did just that with great apology. Then they begged him to let them go. Old Man Stan thought a moment, weighing the outcome, and finally said, "I'll let y'all go, but you gotta hand over all them fish y'all done scooped up illegally from my slough, and then y'all better move yourselves outta here and squat on another part of the river!"

It was agreed to, so now Old Man Stan had enough fish in his freezer to last the winter, not to mention he didn't have to worry about getting seasick for a while, 'til some other speedy wisecracker decided to move into his terrain.

OLD MAN STAN'S BEER BATTERED CATFISH

2 cups vegetable oil

1 cup beer

Juice of 1 lemon

1 cup flour

1 teaspoon salt

1/2 teaspoon black pepper

1 teaspoon Tony Chachere's Cajun Seasoning

12 small catfish fillets

Heat oil in a large, heavy skillet. In a large bowl, combine beer, lemon juice, flour, salt, pepper, and seasoning. Mix well. Dip fillets in batter to coat. Drop battered fish into hot oil. Fry until golden brown. Drain cooked fish on paper towels.

CATFISH CHOWDER

2 cups precooked and shredded catfish fillets

Salt and pepper

1 tablespoon diced bacon or salt pork

1 small onion, chopped

1 cup cooked tomatoes

1 cup diced potatoes

2 cups water

1 tablespoon butter

2 chicken flavor bouillon cubes

Precook the catfish by baking it in a buttered baking pan in a 375° oven until the flesh is white and flaky. Season lightly with salt and pepper.

In a separate frying pan, brown the bacon. Add onions and sauté until lightly brown. Add tomatoes, potatoes, water, butter, and bouillon cubes. Cover. Simmer over medium heat until vegetables are tender. Season to taste with additional salt and pepper. Add catfish and serve at once.

UNCLE DALE'S ALLIGATOR GAR PATTIES

Peanut oil for deep frying

2 pounds alligator gar meat

4 eggs

1 (13-ounce) box instant mashed potatoes

1/2 cup self-rising flour

2 bunches green onions, finely chopped

Salt and pepper

Heat 1/4 inch oil in a frying pan over medium heat. In a large bowl, mix all ingredients together except the oil. Mixture will be stiff. Form into palm-size patties. Dip each patty in flour to coat lightly. Deep fry until golden brown on both sides.

UNCLE PERRY'S SHRIMP PIE

2 cups peeled shrimp (canned or fresh)

1 eggplant, chopped into small chunks

1 white onion, finely chopped

2 apples, coarsely chopped

1/4 cup butter

1 cup crushed saltine crackers

1/2 cup grated mozzarella cheese

Sauté shrimp, eggplant, onion, and apples in butter. Spread cooked mixture into a greased baking pan, then sprinkle with crackers and cheese. Bake for 20 minutes at 350°.

UNCLE DALE'S SHRIMP CREOLE

Corn oil for frying

1 bell pepper, finely chopped

2 yellow onions, finely chopped

2 bunches green onions, finely chopped

4 to 6 cloves garlic, finely chopped

1 stalk celery, finely chopped

3/4 cup corn oil

1/2 cup self-rising flour

2 (14-ounce) cans tomato sauce

1 cup water

3 pounds peeled shrimp

3 tablespoons sugar

1 cup chopped fresh tomatoes

4 bay leaves

In a deep skillet, heat 1/2 inch of corn oil. Sauté bell peppers, yellow onions, green onions, garlic, and celery until wilted. Set aside.

In a separate skillet, make a roux with 3/4

cup corn oil and 1/2 cup self-rising flour. Stir constantly until dark brown. Add 2 cans tomato sauce. Stir in 1 cup of water to the base. Simmer on low heat for 20 minutes.

Add sautéed shrimp and vegetable mixture, plus sugar. Add fresh tomatoes and bay leaves. Simmer for 15 minutes on low heat. Serve with white rice.

CRAB ÉTOUFFÉE

1/4 cup flour

1/3 cup vegetable oil

2 onions, chopped

1 bell pepper, chopped

1/4 cup chopped celery

2 pounds crab meat

1/4 cup chopped green onions

1 tablespoon parsley

1/4 cup water

Salt and pepper

1 teaspoon Tony Chachere's Cajun Seasoning

In a large skillet, brown flour in oil. Add onions, bell pepper, and celery. Cook until wilted. Add crab meat, green onions, parsley, water, and seasonings. Bring to a boil and cook for 15 minutes. Serve with white rice.

CAJUN CRAB MOLD

1 (14-ounce) can mushroom soup

2 (3-ounce) envelopes unflavored gelatin

3 tablespoons cold water

1 pound crab meat, fresh or canned

1 cup mayonnaise

1 (8-ounce) package cream cheese

1 cup chopped green onions

Salt and pepper

1 teaspoon Tony Chachere's Cajun Seasoning

Dash Louisiana Hot Sauce

In a large saucepan, heat mushroom soup until dissolved. Add gelatin, which has been mixed with 3 tablespoons water. Add remaining ingredients and mix well. Pour into three molds and refrigerate overnight. Serve with crackers.

CHAPTER 3

HUNTING IN THE SWAMP: WILD GAME

DEER IN THE BUCKET

Some of the boys were off on a hunting trip way out in the swamp and they ran out of potted meat and Twinkies, but were determined not to leave the woods 'til they shot that big buck they could show off at the boat landing when they got back to civilization. But after ten hours of hunger, one of the boys went into the woods and shot the first deer he saw and brought it back to the campsite.

While they were cleaning the deer meat, Uncle Perry scooped up an old bucket that he saw floating down river. Then he dug through their supplies and found aluminum foil, salt and pepper, and a lone onion. He doctored up that deer roast, wrapped it with foil and put it in the bucket at the edge of the hot coals, and let it cook a few hours while the other guys went back into the woods one last time to try and shoot that twelve-point somebody claimed to have let get away.

When they returned to the campsite empty handed, they ate "Deer in the Bucket" and somebody said, "Bambi here was pretty durn good. The heck with that twelve-point. Let's get on home fore the wives send out a search party."

UNIVERSAL WILD GAME STEW

2 pounds wild game meat of choice,
cut into 1-inch cubes

Whole milk

Flour

Salt and pepper

Oil

1 tablespoon garlic, minced

1 large onion, chopped

1 stalk celery, chopped

1 bunch green onions, finely chopped

Marinate meat in milk, in refrigerator, for 3 hours or overnight if possible to tenderize. Remove meat from milk; do not rinse. Dredge meat in flour to which you've added salt and pepper. In a heavy stockpot, fry meat lightly in a little oil until golden brown on both sides. Add enough water to cover meat. Add garlic, onion, celery, and green onions. Simmer over low heat until meat and vegetables are tender. This stew will make its own gravy. Stir occasionally to keep it from sticking to pot. Serve over rice.

UNCLE PERRY'S DEER IN THE BUCKET

1 (5- to 6-pound) venison roast

Salt and pepper to taste

1 onion, chopped

Season the venison with salt and pepper and chopped onion. Wrap in aluminum foil and place the wrapped roast in a bucket. Set the bucket at the edge of a campfire for 2 to 3 hours.

RIVER CAMP STEW

2 pounds pork, cut into 1-inch cubes

1 fat hen, cut into serving portions

2 pounds deer meat, cut into 1-inch cubes

1 lemon

6 onions

1 bottle ketchup

1 cup mayonnaise

Salt and pepper

2 (14-ounce) cans tomato

12 medium potatoes

1 (8-ounce) jar mustard

1/2 cup Worcestershire sauce

Place cut-up meat in a large, heavy soup pot, and add enough water to cover it. Boil meat until very tender. Remove from pot; use a fork to remove the meat from the bones and shred it finely. Return meat to pot. Add other ingredients. Simmer slowly for 1 hour. May be served immediately.

LOUISIANA VENISON PARMIGIANA

4 (8-ounce) venison steaks

Milk

2 eggs

Salt and pepper

4 tablespoons grated Parmesan cheese

3/4 cup bread crumbs

6 tablespoons olive oil

1 (8-ounce) can tomato sauce

Seasoned salt

Tony Chachere's Cajun Seasoning

3/4 pound mozzarella cheese, sliced

In the refrigerator, marinate venison overnight in milk to tenderize it.

In a mixing bowl, beat eggs. Add salt, pepper, and Parmesan cheese. Dip venison into egg mixture and roll in bread crumbs. In a large skillet, sauté venison steaks in hot olive oil until both sides are brown. Place venison steaks into a baking dish that is large enough so that steaks do not overlap. Cover with tomato sauce. Add seasoned salt and Tony Chachere's Cajun Seasoning. Place slices of mozzarella cheese on each steak and bake at 350° for 15 to 20 minutes.

LOUISIANA
SWEET AND SOUR NUTRIA

NOTE: Nutria (or coypu) are large, herbivorous mammals that live in the marshes and wetlands of Bayou Country. They resemble beaver and are hunted for their pelts and meat.

1 pound nutria meat, cut into 1/2-inch cubes

Cooking oil

1 cup beef bouillon

Salt to taste

1 bell pepper, sliced

2 onions, sliced

1 (14-ounce) can pineapple, drained (reserve syrup, about 1/2 cup)

2 teaspoons soy sauce

1/4 cup sugar

1/4 cup vinegar

3 tablespoons cornstarch

1/4 cup slivered almonds

In a large skillet, brown nutria meat in hot oil. Add bouillon and salt. Cover and simmer for 30 minutes. Add bell pepper, onions, pineapple, soy sauce, pineapple syrup, sugar, vinegar, cornstarch, and almonds. Cook 10 minutes, stirring often, until sauce thickens. Serve on hot rice.

⫷ AS THE RIVER FLOWS ⫸

Some of the hunters were lounging around the camp watching the river flow after a productive morning in the woods, and they got to discussing how they needed to have a big-to-do party on Saturday night, but nobody could think up a good excuse to have a bigger party than they usually do. Then Elroy came up with the bright idea of having a bachelor party. Nobody at the time had any immediate plans of getting married, so Elroy came up with another bright idea—a divorce party, because a few of the guys had mentioned getting one. Although when Elroy mentioned divorce during a sober part of the afternoon, nobody spoke up, especially Dook who was married to Big Bertha.

Elroy said, "Come on, Dook, you been wantin' a divorce for years! Here's your chance!"

Dook just shook his head and said, "Man, you crazy, Elroy. If word gets out that we're gonna be havin' a divorce party on my behalf, y'all be havin' a funeral party after Big Bertha gets through with me!" Well, that shot that bright idea right out the water.

Jimbo uttered, "Y'all can throw me a divorce party."

Then Elroy responded, "You ain't even married this year, Jimbo."

Jimbo replied, "But, next time I get married, y'all will have me covered."

That settled that. The party was on. Then Scooter stipulated, "But this time, don't give Gator no moonshine, 'cause LouAnn told me she'd skin my hide if her old man ended up in prison again after one of them bright idea river parties Elroy dreamt up after a big hunt."

(See my first *Swamp Cookin'* cookbook to get the scoop on Gator and LouAnn.)

BIG MAMA'S
DEER ROAST SURPRISE

1 deer roast, cut from hindquarter

1/2 pound bacon, cut in pieces

5 or 6 cloves garlic, slivered

Salt and pepper

3 tablespoons bacon drippings

1/2 cup butter

1 cup burgundy wine

1 cup sherry

1 large bay leaf

2 tablespoons minced parsley

1 stalk celery, chopped

1 cup whole baby carrots

2 onions, chopped

1/2 cup chopped bell peppers

Tony Chachere's Creole Seasoning

1 (10-ounce) can beef broth

1 cup chicken broth

Cornstarch

With a sharp knife, cut slits into surface of roast. Push pieces of raw bacon and slivers of garlic into these slits to flavor the roast and make it moist. Season the roast with salt and pepper.

In a large skillet, heat the bacon drippings. Place the roast in the pan and brown on all sides.

In a separate skillet, melt the butter. Add remaining ingredients, except broth and cornstarch. Simmer 10 minutes and pour over roast. Cover roast and bake at 350° until roast is tender (about 2 hours). Remove roast from pan. Add beef and chicken broth and enough cornstarch to make a gravy. Serve with rice.

DEER MEAT PIE

1 pound ground deer meat

1 small onion, chopped

2 cloves garlic, chopped

Oil

1 (14-ounce) can mixed vegetables, drained

Salt and pepper

Seasoned salt

2 (10-ounce) cans cream of mushroom soup

2 (9-inch) prepared unbaked pie crusts

In a skillet, brown ground deer meat, onions, and garlic in a small amount of oil until meat is done. Add drained vegetables and seasonings. Add cream of mushroom soup and mix well. Pour mixture into pie crust. Cover pie with second crust. Bake at 350°, until crust is browned.

DEER CURRY WITH RICE

8 small (5-ounce) deer steaks, thinly sliced

2 cups milk

2 tablespoons plus 2 teaspoons curry powder

Salt and pepper

2 tablespoons vegetable oil

1/4 cup flour

1 cup water

2 green bell peppers, sliced

1 large onion, chopped

In refrigerator, marinate deer meat in milk and 2 tablespoons curry for 4 hours or overnight to tenderize. Remove from marinade, but do not rinse. Season with salt and pepper. In a large saucepan, brown deer meat in oil. Add flour and make a roux. When roux is medium brown, add water, bell peppers, onions, and 2 teaspoons curry powder. Simmer for 1 hour over medium-low heat or until meat is done. Stir occasionally to keep from sticking. Add more water if mixture dries out. Add seasonings to taste. Serve over rice.

RED NECK GRAVY

1/2 cup oil

1 cup flour

1/2 onion, finely chopped

1 (14-ounce) can tomato sauce

1 (8-ounce) can tomato paste

Salt and pepper

In a cast-iron skillet, heat oil. Add flour to make a roux. Add onions. Cook till roux is medium brown and onions are soft. Add tomato sauce and paste. Add water until gravy is thin. Salt and pepper to taste and simmer 10 minutes. Serve over cooked rice.

QUAIL JAMBALAYA

10 quails (1 to 3 pounds each)

Salt and pepper

1/4 cup vegetable oil

2 onions, chopped

1 bunch green onions, chopped

1 cup chopped bell peppers

2 tablespoons chopped parsley

2 cups uncooked rice

Season quails with salt and pepper. In deep pot, brown quails in oil. Add 1/2 cup water to pot. Continue cooking. When water evaporates, add another 1/2 cup of water. Stir and continue to add water when needed until gravy turns dark brown. Add onions and then add more water. When water cooks down, add 1 quart of water. Cover and simmer until quails are tender. Adjust seasonings if needed. Add green onions, bell peppers, and parsley. Bring to a boil. Add rice. (There should be twice as much water as there is rice.) Cover and simmer approximately 15 minutes until rice is done. Stir and serve.

〜 THE VOODOO SHACK 〜

Scoot and Tex had been duck hunting early one morning and it was getting about time to meet at the boat when Scoot fired his gun a couple times, like they had practiced in case one of them got lost or hurt. Tex hurried through the swamp and found Scoot at the edge of the slough on all fours, sick as a dog.

"You got the flu or somethin'?" Tex asked.

"No, I done stepped into that moccasin bed over there and got bit. I don't think I can make it to a hospital, so you gotta get me to Wild Wanda's shack downstream."

So Tex hauled Scoot to the little remote shack sitting on the bayou.

Tex had never met Wild Wanda, but he had heard about her, and he was quite surprised to see the short, roundish woman with jet black hair and a crow on her shoulder. She wasn't that bad looking either. Wild Wanda could tell right away what the problem was and told Tex to put Scoot on her feather bed and remove his pants. Wild Wanda sucked the snake venom from his leg and then told Tex to wait outside while she did her magic.

So Tex stepped outside and had a seat on a cypress stump 'til all that commotion was over.

An hour later, Scoot emerged grinning like a fool. At first Tex didn't pry, he was just glad to see his friend alive and well. But while they tromped back to the boat, Tex finally said, "Man, say somethin'."

So Scoot confessed, "I tell you what, Tex, you won't find that kinda treatment in town for a snakebite!" Then of course he went into great detail about Wild Wanda's voodoo swamp antidotes.

Wouldn't you know, just the next hunting trip, Tex stepped into the same moccasin bed that Scoot had stepped in.

DUCK LUCK

Salt and pepper

4 wild ducks (3 to 5 pounds each)

2 large onions, halved

Oil

2 (10-ounce) cans chicken broth

Orange Wine Sauce (see recipe this page)

Salt and pepper cleaned ducks. Put half an onion inside each duck. In a heavy skillet, brown the ducks on all sides in a little vegetable oil. Remove ducks from skillet and set aside. Pour excess grease out of skillet and add chicken broth and Orange Wine Sauce. Simmer for a few minutes.

Place ducks in a large roasting pan. Baste with broth/Orange Wine Sauce mixture and add all of this mixture to the pan. Cover and simmer for 3 hours over medium heat. Serve Duck Luck over white or "dirty" rice.

ORANGE WINE SAUCE

3 oranges

2 tablespoons butter

1/4 cup light corn syrup

1 tablespoon honey

1/4 cup white wine

Peel oranges and cut into 1/8-inch slices. In a skillet, heat butter over medium heat until melted. Stir in corn syrup, honey, and wine. Bring to a boil. Add oranges and reduce heat. Simmer, uncovered, for 25 minutes to thicken the sauce. Stir constantly.

WILD DUCK GUMBO

3/4 cup flour

3/4 cup peanut oil

1 large onion, chopped

2 large (3 to 5 pounds each) wild ducks, skinned and quartered

3 quarts water

2 tablespoons salt

1 tablespoon black pepper

1/4 cup chopped green onions

1/4 cup chopped cilantro

1/4 cup chopped parsley

Filé powder to taste

In a large stockpot, prepare a dark brown roux with flour and oil. Sauté onions in roux until tender. Add duck. Cover and cook for 5 minutes. Drain off excess grease. Slowly add water, stirring with roux. Add remaining seasonings, except for parsley and filé powder. Cover and simmer for 3 hours or until meat is tender. Add parsley and serve with white rice. Filé to taste.

DUCK À LA KING

3 cups cooked duck meat

6 tablespoons butter

1 large sweet onion, chopped

2 stalks celery, chopped

6 tablespoons flour

3 cups whole milk

1 chicken bouillon cube

Salt

Pepper

French bread, freshly baked

Either precook a medium (4-pound) duck, or use leftover roast duck meat. Remove meat from bones and shred. Set aside.

In a large skillet, melt butter. Add onion and celery and cook until tender. Add flour and mix well. Add milk slowly, while stirring. Add bouillon cube, salt, and pepper.

Add shredded duck meat to pan and simmer 15 minutes. Serve over French bread.

SWEET DUCKS

Salt and pepper

4 ducks, whole, cleaned

1 apple, sliced

1 cup chopped celery

1/2 onion, chopped

Butter for browning

2 cups vermouth

1 cup orange juice

3 ounces brandy

3 tablespoons Worcestershire sauce

1 orange, sliced

Salt and pepper ducks. Stuff ducks with apples, celery, and onions. In a large skillet, brown each duck in melted butter. Place ducks in baking pan, breast side up. Add vermouth and small amount of water. Cover and bake at 300° for 2 1/2 hours. Remove and cool. Save liquids. Debone ducks and place in casserole dish. Add reserved liquid, orange juice, brandy, and Worcestershire sauce. Cover with orange slices. Bake uncovered at 275° for 45 minutes. Serve over white or brown rice.

GLAZED MALLARDS

2 mallard ducks, whole, cleaned

1/2 teaspoon salt

1/4 teaspoon ground pepper

1 1/4 cups dry sherry

3 tablespoons dark brown sugar

1 1/2 tablespoons peanut oil

Place ducks in baking dish. Season with salt and pepper. In a saucepan, combine sherry with brown sugar and oil. Stir over medium heat until sugar is melted. Pour sherry mixture over ducks. Cover and marinate for 2 hours; you should turn the ducks to soak both sides. Bake ducks for 1 hour at 350°, basting every 15 minutes.

ᜒ 00-7 ᜒ

If you see him pass by in his antique speed boat, you'd swear he was legal—at a distance. But if you get up close and personal and look behind his mirrored sunglasses, you'd behold his keen eyes observing you with a superior swampman glance. 00-7 has been a resident of the swamp so long that he's befriended the Honey Island Swamp Monster, among a few other wild things. If he takes a notion to talk to you, you'll know he's harmless unless you mess with him or his dog. You can only get to his place by boat, and if you're not invited, don't show up unless it's daylight and he can see you coming. You wouldn't want to get caught in one of his boobie-traps. I asked 00-7 how he got his nickname and he just grinned, so another swamp outlaw who was sitting nearby said, "He got to chasing one of them river rats in a boat and drove right on through the cypress trees 'til he became airborne like James Bond does in the movies."

I asked 00-7 why he lives way back in the secluded swamp and he said, "I had to get away from a woman."

That pretty much summed it up that day, but on another occasion, when 00-7 was in the mood to elaborate, he told me that he had promised himself that he'd stay out of trouble—the kind of trouble usually caused by a woman. So when he got out of the jail house, that meant he'd have to move out of town, and the swamp was as far out of town as it gets. After a moment of silence while 00-7 reflected on what he just said, he quickly pointed out, "But that don't mean I don't like women no more. I just stay away from the ones in town!"

OUTLAW DEER LOAF

1 pound ground deer meat

1/2 pound ground beef

1 large onion, chopped

1 bell pepper, chopped

1/2 cup crumbled stale French bread

1 egg

1 teaspoon Tony Chachere's Creole Seasoning

1 bulb garlic, finely chopped

Dash Louisiana Hot Sauce

1 teaspoon salt

1/2 teaspoon pepper

Mix together all ingredients. Bake at 350° in meat-loaf pan for 1 hour or until done.

⚘ BLUE EYES ⚘

Another outlaw that secludes himself in the swamp is Blue Eyes, who is the most dangerous of all, because he is a legal outlaw. He has papers from government people to prove it. In the old days, as Blue Eyes calls them, he'd only come around once in a blue moon, and when he did, he'd pull out a roll of cash—the size you see in gangster movies. He'd gas up his pick-up truck and his boat, tell a few adventuresome tales, drink a few beers, take a boat ride, tell a few more tales, and off he'd go again 'til another blue moon. But after Blue Eyes got his legal papers from the government people— after serving a few years in various penitentiaries around the country, he kind of settled down a bit, 'til he shot a few rednecks down at a local saloon.

I asked Blue Eyes how he got away with shooting those rednecks right there in town where everybody could see and he said, "'Cause they shot me first. I got the bullet holes right here to prove it." He pointed them out to me.

Then I asked Blue Eyes why he chose the swamp to retire and he said, "I didn't, it chose me, and by the way, I ain't retired yet. I got a few other matters to take care of one day."

SWAMP OUTLAW PATÉ

4 pounds wild boar livers (or raised hog liver),
ground

2 pounds pork fat, ground

3 pounds pork meat, ground

8 cloves garlic, minced

3 tablespoons salt

2 tablespoons black pepper

1 teaspoon red pepper

1 tablespoon Tony Chachere's Cajun Seasoning

Using a food processor or sausage grinder, grind liver, meat, and fat all together. Put in a large, deep pot. Add garlic, other seasonings, and 4 cups of water, and stir. Cook over medium heat until fat rises to top, stirring constantly. When mixture is thoroughly cooked (no pink shows), pour into canning jars and refrigerate. The fat will rise to the top of each jar to seal it. Serve with crackers or French bread. The paté will keep for several days if refrigerated.

RABBIT SOUP DE JOUR

2 cups okra, sliced into 1/2-inch segments

1/3 cup olive oil

2 cups chopped red onions

1 bell pepper, chopped

3 quarts water

1 pound rabbit, cut up

1 teaspoon curry powder

1/2 teaspoon ground ginger

Salt and pepper

1/2 cup chopped green onions, for garnish

In a large soup pot, smother okra by sautéing it in a small amount of oil until golden brown.

Add onions and bell pepper; sauté until tender. Add water. Simmer this vegetable mixture while browning rabbit.

In a separate large skillet, brown rabbit in oil. When meat is cooked, add it to the vegetable soup mixture. Add seasonings. Garnish with green onions just before serving. Serve over rice.

⚜ THE LOST SWAMP REBEL ⚜

The Lost Swamp Rebel isn't a wanted man—at the moment—but there was a rumor one time that he slid out of a police car window when nobody was looking and romped off through the marsh on foot because he had to check his crawfish traps.

At the time we all supposed the cops were awful embarrassed for leaving the rear window down. A bunch of gossip was relayed up and down the river that the city cops had a major point to prove with getaway artists. The first point was they claimed the Lost Swamp Rebel was armed and dangerous. But it'd be awful hard to be dangerous without a gun and a boat. Not to mention he was handcuffed—but that matter was taken care of when one of them alligators that he had to wrestle with on occasion bit the handcuffs right off. Then it was determined that he managed to patch up an old abandoned skiff and was able to check his crawfish traps before nightfall and had enough food supply to last a few days, 'til that crazy business blew over, but it didn't. Those cops were looking up and down the river peering behind cypress trees 'til sundown.

Not too many rational outsiders stay in the swamp after dark, so that's when the Lost Swamp Rebel would come out for socializing with a few River People who were wrongfully accused of being his accomplices. All they were doing were lounging around shooting the bull and boiling crawfish like they always do. But during one of those crawfish boils, the Lost Swamp Rebel was reminded what happened to poor old C.J. years back. So he turned himself in.

FROG LEG DUMPLINGS

3 pounds frog leg meat

1 onion, chopped

2 cups flour

1/4 cup oil

1 egg

1/2 teaspoon baking soda

1/2 teaspoon salt

1 cup buttermilk

1 (10-ounce) can cream of chicken soup

1 teaspoon Tony Chachere's Cajun Seasoning

1 cup milk

In a stockpot, boil frog legs in salted water with onion until tender. Remove legs from pot and save broth.

When legs are cool enough to handle, remove the meat from the bones, using a fork.

In a mixing bowl, make dumpling dough with flour, oil, egg, baking soda, salt, and buttermilk. Roll out the dough 1/2 inch thick and cut into circles with a dumpling cutter or a drinking glass that has been dipped in flour.

Return the shredded frog meat to hot broth and add cream of chicken soup. Bring to a rolling boil. Add Cajun seasoning. Drop dumplings, one at a time, into the boiling broth. Reduce heat to medium and cook for about 15 minutes. Add milk; allow broth to return to a boil. Cook for an additional 5 minutes or until the dumplings are thoroughly cooked.

FROG LEGS
FIRST CLASS

12 frog legs

1/2 cup butter

1 cup white wine

1/4 cup sliced onions

1 teaspoon minced garlic

1/4 teaspoon salt

1/4 teaspoon white pepper

1 teaspoon chopped cilantro

1 teaspoon tarragon

1 teaspoon rosemary

In a frying pan, sauté frog legs in butter until lightly browned. Add wine, onions, garlic, salt, white pepper, and cilantro. Cover and simmer over low heat for 20 minutes. Add tarragon and rosemary and simmer for an additional 15 minutes, or until meat is tender.

⚜ SWAMP MASTER ⚜

Swamp Master, alias Denty Crawford, is not really an outlaw, but the legend isn't surprising, since he is one of the first swamp settlers. Swamp Master served time, too, but not in jail—in 'Nam.

Swamp Master can be classified dangerous in the swamp if you challenge him. That means don't swim in dangerous waters unless you don't mind drowning. He has been tracking the swamplands all his life, knows the ins and outs of the nooks and sloughs, and on numerous occasions has been summoned by the authorities to find lost hunters. He is a friend to the River People who like hanging out at his swamp villa listening to war stories and swamp stories that could be put on that show "Believe It or Not."

When Swamp Master isn't running trotlines and cooking, he's out in the swamp collecting driftwood and other souvenirs, like swamp critters. He keeps certain skeletons of the ones that nearly took his life—like a giant turtle head that hangs on his wall to commemorate the day it lunged at his throat. Thank goodness for the trotline that yanked it back, giving it just enough room to get a mouthful of his beard.

If you look in the outside icebox, you'll see a whole bunch of other swamp critters that all have a tale behind their capture. Swamp Master told me that I can tell you his real name and use his picture because he's not afraid of anything except the Honey Island Swamp Monster, which he got a good look at on one of his swamp expeditions.

ALLIGATOR
CACCIATORE

6 pounds alligator meat, cubed into 1-inch pieces

1 (8-ounce) bottle of Italian dressing

1/2 cup olive oil

4 onions, sliced

4 cloves garlic, minced

2 (8-ounce) cans tomato sauce

1/2 teaspoon crushed oregano

1/2 cup sauterne

2 (1-pound) cans tomatoes

2 teaspoons salt

1 teaspoon celery seed

2 bay leaves

1 (1-pound) package spaghetti, prepared according to package directions

In the refrigerator, marinate alligator meat for at least 4 hours in Italian dressing.

Heat olive oil in a large skillet and add alligator meat. Brown slowly on both sides. Remove gator meat from skillet and cook onions and garlic until tender. In a separate bowl, combine remaining ingredients for sauce. Return gator meat to skillet and add sauce mixture. Cover and simmer for 45 minutes on low heat. Discard bay leaves. Cool. Serve over spaghetti.

ALLIGATOR CHILE

8 ounces boiled alligator meat

1 (6-ounce) can tomato sauce

1 (14-ounce) can stewed tomatoes

Chili powder

Salt and pepper

In a deep skillet, mix everything together. Bring to a boil, then reduce heat and simmer 2 hours. Serve with crackers.

SCOOTER'S GOLDEN GATOR NUGGETS

5 pounds of gator meat, cut into 1-inch cubes

1 (8-ounce) bottle of Italian dressing

1 cup milk

3 eggs

Salt and pepper

1/2 teaspoon sugar

1 teaspoon Tony Chachere's Cajun Seasoning

1 cup cornmeal

Peanut oil for deep frying

In the refrigerator, marinate chunks of gator meat in Italian dressing overnight or, if you can't wait that long, for at least 3 hours.

In a mixing bowl, make a wet batter with milk, eggs, salt and pepper, sugar, and Tony Chachere's Cajun Seasoning to taste.

Pour cornmeal into a separate container and add salt, pepper, and Tony Chachere's Cajun Seasoning to taste; shake well.

Heat peanut oil in deep pot or deep-fat fryer. Remove gator meat from Italian dressing and put into wet batter. Roll the meat in dry cornmeal, drop in hot oil, and fry until golden brown on all sides. Remove golden gator nuggets and serve with ketchup or on bread with desired dressing.

TERRAL'S GATOR BOBS

5 pounds alligator meat, cut into 2-inch cubes

1 (8-ounce) bottle Italian dressing

24 whole mushrooms

3 large onions, quartered

3 large bell peppers, quartered

3 cups milk

3 eggs

1 teaspoon salt

1 teaspoon pepper

1 teaspoon Tony Chachere's Cajun Seasoning

2 cups flour

Peanut oil for deep frying

In the refrigerator, marinate cubed alligator meat in Italian dressing for at least 4 hours or overnight if possible. Thread meat onto shish-kabob sticks, alternating with mushrooms, onions, and bell peppers.

In a mixing bowl, make a wet batter with milk, eggs, 1/2 teaspoon salt, 1/2 teaspoon pepper, and 1/2 teaspoon Tony Chachere's Cajun Seasoning. In a separate bowl, combine flour and remaining salt, pepper, and Tony Chachere's Cajun Seasoning.

Heat oil in a deep pot or deep-fat fryer to 375°.

Dip gator bobs into the wet batter first, then into the dry, seasoned flour mixture. Deep fry each gator bob in hot oil until golden brown.

JOHNNY'S 11-FOOT ALLIGATOR GUMBO

2¹/₂ pounds of alligator meat from an 11-foot alligator, cubed into 2-inch pieces (if an 11-footer is not available, a smaller gator will do)

2 pounds smoked sausage, removed from casings and chopped

2 cups chopped onion

1 cup chopped celery

1 cup chopped bell pepper

4 cloves garlic, chopped

¹/₄ cup vegetable oil

3 (14-ounce) cans stewed tomatoes

1 (14-ounce) can Italian-style tomato sauce

¹/₂ cup red wine

2 cups chopped okra

1 tablespoon parsley

2 bay leaves

1 tablespoon Tony Chachere's Creole Seasoning

1 teaspoon salt

1 teaspoon black pepper

1/2 teaspoon garlic salt

2 pints raw oysters

1 (16-ounce) package rigatoni pasta

1 pound shrimp, deveined and peeled

In a large pot, sauté alligator meat and sausage with onion, celery, bell pepper, and garlic in vegetable oil until alligator meat is tender. Add tomatoes and tomato sauce and bring to a boil. Add wine, okra, and seasonings. Add water if mixture is too thick. Reduce heat and simmer for 10 minutes. Add oysters and pasta to pot. When noodles are almost tender, add shrimp. Cook until shrimp are pink.

❧ BRIAN'S SWAMP SURVIVAL FOOD ❧

If you ever get lost in the wilderness, Mother Nature can provide a meal—if you know what to look for and how to prepare it. You must be very careful what you pick to eat in the wild because some plants are poisonous. Brian says that you can also eat "wild" even if you're not lost because it tastes good.

Cattail roots are a good survival food. These reedy plants usually grow near the edge of a swamp or pond and have big dark brown heads that look like cigars. The roots look like potatoes and make a tasty vegetable. You must boil the root until it is soft, then slice and eat it. If you are somewhere that you have supplies, you can season cattail root with salt, pepper, and butter. It's very tasty.

CHAPTER 4

LIFE ON THE RIVER: STICK TO THE RIBS SOUPS AND STEWS

PEANUT BUTTER ON THE GRAPEVINE

Judy ran into Sam at the supermarket and noticed that he had a whole basket full of peanut butter. She asked him who in the world was going to be eating all that peanut butter.

He grinned that wanna-be sexy grin of his and said, "Who says we gonna eat it all? You wanna come help me spread it?"

Right away Judy assumed Sam was going to do something kinky with that peanut butter and she didn't ask any more questions, mostly out of embarrassment, but as soon as she spun into Martha's yard, the grapevine started growing. Martha knew by the way the truck door was opened before the engine cut off, the news was bound to be good. She swung open the screen door and yelled, "What'd you hear, Judy?"

Already out of breath, just from the excitement of the information, Judy exhaled, "Martha, you just wouldn't believe who I saw in the supermarket just then."

"Tell me, hun!"

The two women went inside to prepare the neighborhood

newsletter. While Martha fixed a fresh pot of coffee, Judy sketched out the saga. "Who you reckon he's gonna be smearing that peanut butter all over tonight?"

Martha quickly blurted out the name, "Sally Ann!"

"Why you know it, girl. Sally Ann always did bring peanut butter sandwiches to school and share 'em with the Joe brothers under the bleachers at recess. I knew she was a little on the wild side."

As the day went on, the protein from that peanut butter made that grapevine grow and grow, and you can just imagine what else went into Judy and Martha's morning column that got delivered around the neighborhood by noon. When it landed on Bobby Joe's kitchen table, he almost fell out the chair with laughter.

His wife Thelma wanted to know what was so durn funny about it. He turned to the three women and said, "Thelma, hun, it ain't Sally Ann that's gonna be making peanut butter sandwiches tonight. Sam's taking that peanut butter to the deer camp so we can lure 'em over in droves."

Thelma responded, "Bobby Joe, you best be explaining that more clearly."

Bobby Joe got up from the table shaking his head and said, "Y'all women will find any durn thing to gossip 'bout. Y'all should go find yourselves something resourceful to do."

So Thelma responded, "And do you have any suggestions, Mr. Smart Butt?"

Bobby Joe answered, "Yeah, if y'all can smear that peanut butter on the cypress trees in the swamp quick as y'all smeared it on the grapevine this morning, then them deer will be plentiful when hunting season opens next week."

The three women stood there, still unsure of his point. Then Thelma turned to Martha and Judy and said, "There's something suspicious going on up there at that deer camp."

Bobby Joe went to the camp to tell the men what kind of rumors got launched in the 'hood that morning. They had themselves a good laugh. Sam will have a lot of explaining to do to his new old lady, who knows nothing about deer hunting and peanut butter.

NANA'S PORK CHOP AND TURNIP STEW

4 or 5 pork chops

Cooking oil

1 onion, chopped

2 cloves garlic, minced

1 tablespoon flour

1 (10-ounce) can chicken broth

1/2 cup water

8 turnips, diced 1/2 inch thick

Salt and pepper

1/4 cup chopped green onions

Brown pork chops in oil with chopped onions and garlic. Remove meat, onions, and garlic. Make a roux with a tablespoon of flour in the same pan. When roux is dark brown, return garlic and onions to the pan. Add chicken broth and water. Return pork chops to pan. Add turnips, salt and pepper to taste, and green onions. Cook over medium heat for 1 hour or until turnips are soft.

❧ SWAMP CHATTER ❧

There isn't anything more entertaining than a bunch of swamp chatter from a flock of swamp birds lurking in the cypress trees at the crack of dawn, who are just a cackling about stories they heard from the night owls about what took place at the river camps after sundown. Now let's get the record straight once and for all.

The one accused of trying to steal Mrs. Know-It-All's old man at the Squirrel Hunt Festivity, wouldn't take him if she handed him over on a crawfish platter. The one that did steal him wants to give him back.

That woman you heard was with so 'n' so last weekend, wasn't; that was somebody else. And the cute one you suspect left with what's-his-name, did, but not for the reason you thought— she got a boat ride back to the boat landing before somebody at the camp got a black eye.

The young lady you heard about dancing on the picnic table was doing no such a thing. She used the picnic table to make a quick getaway from the fool making a pass at her. The headlines that went out about the widow kissing you-know-who, didn't mean nothing by it except a friendly hello.

Who the heck started that rumor about that New Orleans woman skinny dipping? She was thrown in the river by her beau and nearly drowned when her dress got hung on a cypress stump and she had to take it off. Now if anybody is so worried about who's cheating who, who's old lady threw them out the house for not coming off the river, and who's going to get their butt kicked, then come hang out at the camp and you will see it's all a bunch of swamp chatter from a flock of swamp birds who don't have anything better to do at daybreak.

LOUISIANA SWAMP RICE

2 dozen chicken livers

2 dozen chicken gizzards

2 tablespoons butter

1 stalk celery, chopped

1/2 cup chopped green onions

1 1/2 cups chopped parsley

1/4 cup bacon grease

2 1/2 pounds white rice

1 chicken bouillon cube

1 teaspoon Tony Chachere's Creole Seasoning

Salt and pepper to taste

Cook livers and gizzards in butter. When cooked, chop gizzards into 1/4-inch dice. Sauté celery, onions, and parsley in bacon grease. Cover pan, reduce heat, and cook for 1 hour. Add gizzards and livers and cook for another 30 minutes. While meat and vegetable mixture cooks, prepare 2 1/2 pounds of white rice with water seasoned with the chicken bouillon cube. When rice is done, mix in meat and vegetable mixture. Season to taste. Mix well.

VIOLA'S OYSTER SOUP

1/2 cup butter

1 cup chopped green onions

2 (10-ounce) cans cream of mushroom soup

1 1/2 cups milk

Salt and pepper

2 cups raw oysters

In a saucepan, sauté butter and chopped green onions. Add cream of mushroom soup. Cook down, stirring constantly. Pour in milk, salt, and pepper, and cook on low until sauce thickens. Drain oysters, but don't rinse. Drop oysters into soup. Cook for 20 minutes on low heat. Serve with crackers.

UNCLE DALE'S OYSTER SOUP

1 pint oysters

1/4 cup corn oil margarine

1 pint water

1 (12-ounce) can evaporated milk

2 cups crushed saltine crackers

Salt and pepper

In a large 3-quart saucepan, heat oysters, margarine, water, and evaporated milk. Simmer for 1 minute over medium heat. Turn heat down; add saltine crackers to mixture. Salt and pepper to taste. Simmer over medium-low heat for 5 minutes, stirring constantly.

NANA'S CRAB STEW

1/3 cup flour

1/4 cup oil

1/2 cup chopped celery

1 large green bell pepper, finely chopped

1 onion, chopped

1 (14-ounce) can chicken or fish broth

Tony Chachere's Cajun Seasoning

1 (14-ounce) can diced tomatoes

Salt and pepper

12 small Louisiana blue crabs, halved, with claws attached

1 pint real crab meat

6 eggs

In a heavy skillet, make a roux with flour and oil. Add celery, green pepper, and onion. Sauté until wilted. Add chicken or fish broth. After mixture comes to a rolling boil, add Cajun spice. Stir in diced tomatoes, salt, and pepper. Add crab halves. Cook for 30 minutes, then add canned crab meat. Break raw eggs onto top of skillet mixture, being careful not to break the yolks. Cover and let eggs cook about 10 minutes, or until they turn yellow and are done. Serve over rice.

SMOKED TURKEY SOUP

1 cup chopped celery

1 cup chopped sweet onions

Olive oil to sauté vegetables

2 cups smoked turkey meat, cut into chunks (this can be
leftover turkey from Thanksgiving)

5 cups water

1 (14-ounce) can stewed tomatoes

1 cup baby carrots

1 tablespoon minced garlic

1/4 cup finely chopped cilantro

1 teaspoon chopped parsley

2 chicken bouillon cubes

1 teaspoon salt

1 teaspoon pepper

1 teaspoon Tony Chachere's Cajun Seasoning

In a large skillet, sauté celery and onions in olive oil until tender. Add
turkey and stir with vegetables for 3 minutes. Add water, stewed tomatoes, carrots, and remaining ingredients. Cook over medium heat for 40
minutes. Serve with white rice or crackers.

NANA'S CHICKEN STEW

1 chicken, cut up

Vegetable oil for browning

1/2 cup flour

1 cup water

1 onion, chopped

1/2 bell pepper, chopped

1 stalk celery, chopped

4 cloves garlic, chopped

Dash hot sauce

1/2 teaspoon Tony Chachere's Cajun Seasoning

Salt and pepper

1 (14-ounce) can chicken broth

In a large skillet, brown chicken in oil. Remove chicken and drain oil into a separate large pot. Make a roux with flour, water, and this same oil. Stir until brown. Add vegetables and seasonings and cook until vegetables are soft. Return chicken to pot and add chicken broth. Cook about 1 hour on medium heat. Serve with white rice.

UNCLE PERRY'S SOUTHERN LENTIL SOUP

1/4 pound lentils

4 cloves garlic, chopped

2 stalks celery, chopped

1 tablespoon olive oil

1 onion, chopped

2 tablespoons soy sauce

Dash hot sauce

Salt and pepper

Rinse lentils thoroughly to remove dust. Combine all ingredients in a large soup pot. Bring to a boil. Cover; reduce heat and simmer for 30 minutes. Serve with crackers.

〰 BIG BERTHA SAVES THE DAY 〰

RayAnn was in the middle of skinning dinner when she went into labor. Her husband, Willis, had gone boar hunting with the other men and they had taken all the boats, so Sara Bell, who was lighting coals in the smoker, had to fetch an old pirogue from behind the camp.

While dragging that pirogue to the water, Sara Bell was just a cursing because RayAnn had no business being in the swamp when she was nine months pregnant. RayAnn was quick to point out that it was hunting season and that she had no choice if she wanted to be with her old man.

So RayAnn climbed into the old pirogue with Sara Bell, and poor old Sara Bell got to paddling quick as she could 'til her in'fo'zema started acting up and she just about collapsed. So RayAnn took over paddling, nearly about ready to pop out that young'un right there on the Pearl River. Luckily they were going downstream.

Just when she couldn't paddle anymore, here came Big Bertha, who was in search of her husband Elroy after she had got wind of a divorce party on his behalf. So RayAnn and Sara Bell climbed into Big Bertha's speed boat and she got them to the emergency room just in time.

When the men returned to the camp with two wild boar, they found a note stuck on a piece of driftwood that read, "RayAnn done went into labor. I hope them hogs were worth it."

Willis grinned and said, "Looks like we got more than one reason to celebrate tonight—we killed two hogs, the coals are hot, and the wives ain't here to gripe."

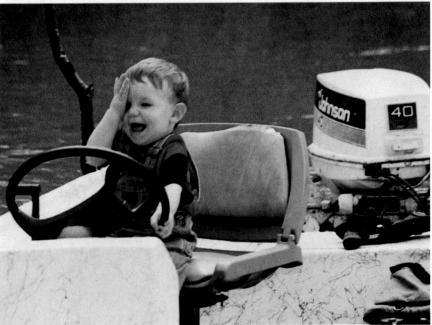

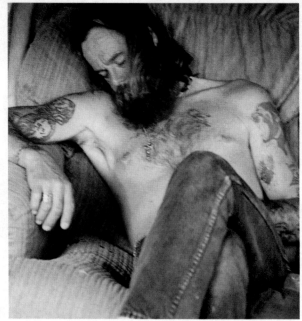

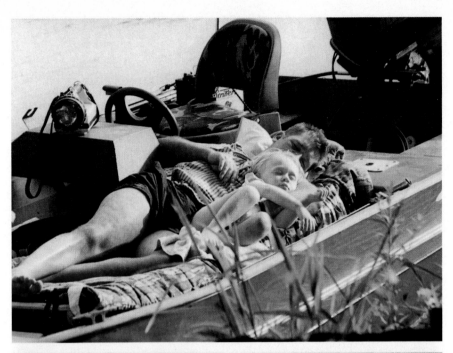

BIG BERTHA'S HUNT YOU DOWN TATER TOES

3 large potatoes, cubed 1/2 inch thick

3 tablespoons butter

1 bunch green onions, minced

1 large red onion, chopped

2 cloves garlic, finely chopped

1 teaspoon Tony Chachere's Cajun Seasoning

1/2 teaspoon salt

1/2 teaspoon pepper

Louisiana Crystal Hot Sauce to taste

Boil potatoes until soft; drain and set aside. Melt butter in a heavy skillet on medium heat. Sauté minced green onions, red onions, and garlic until soft. Add cooked potatoes to skillet. Add dry seasonings, toss gently, and cook on medium heat until potatoes turn golden brown. Season with Crystal Hot Sauce before serving.

YVONNE'S CREOLE POTATO SOUP

6 potatoes, peeled and diced

2 quarts water

1/4 pound bacon

1 onion, chopped

4 stalks celery, chopped

Salt and pepper

Pinch Tony Chachere's Creole Seasoning

1 cup half-and-half cream

Place potatoes in a large soup pot and cover with 2 quarts water. Trim fat off bacon and chop into small pieces. Add bacon to potatoes along with onion, celery, salt, pepper, and Tony Chachere's Creole Seasoning. Cook on medium heat until potatoes are soft. Mash them well in pot. Add half-and-half. Add more water if soup is too thick. Cook an additional 5 minutes.

AUNT SANDY'S HASH BROWN STEW

1 (1-pound) bag frozen hash browns

1 bag Bird's Eye Brand Seasoning Blend

1 (14-ounce) can cheddar cheese soup

1 (14-ounce) can cream of celery soup

1 pound bacon

1 green bell pepper, chopped

1 pint whipping cream

In a saucepan, boil hash browns in a small amount of water until tender (about 30 minutes). Add the seasoning blend, which contains red and green peppers and onions. Stir in cheddar cheese soup and cream of celery soup, adding enough additional water to make a creamy mixture.

In a separate skillet, fry bacon until crisp; remove bacon and drain on paper towels. Add chopped bell pepper to the bacon fat and sauté until tender. Pour the sautéed peppers and remaining bacon fat into the hash browns. Stir in whipping cream just before serving. Garnish each serving with crumbled bacon.

UNCLE DALE'S BROCCOLI SOUP

1 large broccoli head

1 can condensed milk or half-and-half cream

1/2 cup margarine

Salt and pepper

Flour

6 slices American cheese

Break broccoli into small pieces (florets). Peel stalk and cut into thin slices. In a large soup pot, boil broccoli in enough water to cover. Cook until tender. Add condensed milk, margarine, salt, and pepper. Slowly add enough flour to thicken the mixture to a creamy soup consistency. When the soup is as thick as you like, add the American cheese and stir until cheese melts.

UNCLE DALE'S
VEGGIE BURGER SOUP

1 pound ground meat (beef or turkey)

1 large soup bone

2 cups chopped carrots

3 stalks celery, chopped

1 (14-ounce) can green beans

1 (14-ounce) can whole kernel corn

1 (14-ounce) can English peas

1/2 head cabbage, chopped

1 (16-ounce) can whole tomatoes, chopped

Salt and pepper

1/2 pound shell pasta

3 pounds potatoes, wedged

Brown ground meat in a large skillet. Drain excess fat. In a separate large pot, boil soup bone for 30 minutes in enough water to cover. Add vegetables, except for potatoes. Add browned meat, salt, and pepper. Cook over medium heat until vegetables are tender. Add pasta and potatoes. Cook over medium-low heat until potatoes are tender.

UNCLE DALE'S TEN-BEAN SOUP

1/2 pound slab bacon

1 (1-pound) bag ten-bean mixture

Ham shank, cubed

Large ham hock

Black pepper

In a deep soup pot, sauté bacon until crisp. Do not drain off the fat. Add enough water to half fill the pot. Add beans, ham shank, ham hock, and pepper. Simmer until beans are tender and ham comes off the bone. It should be salty enough from the ham hock. If not, add salt to taste. Serve with rice.

CHAPTER 5

THE SPICE OF LIFE: SIDE DISHES AND DESSERTS

 **THE DRUNK NAKED MAN**

Mama was working at her little bait shop near the swamp, when a pick-up truck pulled up and honked. She went out to see who it was and what their problem was. She found an old man sitting at the wheel, not a stitch of clothes on his frail body, and he was drunk as a coot.

He said, "M'am can you please fetch me a six-pack to go?"

Mama told him to wait right there. She went inside to call the Sheriff and said, "Come quick, there's a drunk naked man in my parking lot."

The Sheriff said, "Can you give us a description?"

Mama replied, "He's stark naked, what else do you need to know!"

The Sheriff told Mama to detain him. So she went back outside and tried to make conversation. Mama politely said, "I haven't seen you around here before."

Then he answered, "I'm visiting a lady friend up the road. You wanna come join us?"

The Sheriff arrived just when Mama was running out of things to talk about with an old naked stranger who was trying to make a pass at her, bless his heart. The Sheriff told Mama to go wait inside. So Mama stood at the window and watched the Sheriff and his deputy make the poor old naked man step outside his truck so they could search his vehicle. She had never seen such a pitiful sight.

Since he didn't have a dangerous weapon on him (and that included you-know-what), they let him get back in his truck and they told him to wait right there while they went into the bait shop to ask Mama if she wished to press obscenity charges. She said, "Why no. I just wanted to make sure the poor old soul got home safely."

While the Sheriff and his deputy were chit-chatting and snacking on a couple of Daddy's homemade pickled eggs, the old naked man sped off towards the swamp and was never seen again.

DADDY'S HOMEMADE PICKLED EGGS

1 gallon pickle juice or 1 gallon vinegar

1/2 to 1 cup salt

2 (3-ounce) bags crab boil

3 dozen boiled eggs, peeled

To a gallon of pickle juice, add 1/2 cup salt and 2 bags crab boil. If you don't have a gallon of pickle juice, use 1 gallon of vinegar and add 1 cup of salt and 2 bags crab boil. Add 3 dozen boiled peeled eggs and let them soak for a week or two.

MAMA'S ONION RICE CASSEROLE

1/2 cup rice

1/2 cup butter

1 (3-ounce) package onion soup mix or
1 (10-ounce) can onion soup

1 (10-ounce) can mushroom soup

In a heavy skillet, sauté rice in butter. Add onion soup and mushroom soup. Heat. Pour into casserole dish. Bake, covered, at 350° for 45 minutes.

MAW MAW'S BUTTER BEAN ROUX

Flour

Oil

1 pound butter beans

Salt and pepper

Water

In a saucepan, make roux with flour and oil. Add butter beans, salt, and pepper. Cover with 3 inches of water. Cook down very slowly until beans are tender and gravy thickens. Serve alone or with rice.

MRS. ODILLE'S STUFFED SHRIMP MIRLITON

NOTE: Mirlitons are "vegetable pears," a popular vegetable in Louisiana, and are similar to summer squash or eggplants. If mirlitons aren't available, you can substitute either squash or eggplant for this and the next recipe.

3 mirlitons

1 1/2 dozen shrimp, halved lengthwise

1 tablespoon butter

1 onion, chopped

1 clove garlic, chopped

1 tomato, chopped

1 teaspoon parsley

1 teaspoon thyme

1 bay leaf, minced

Salt and pepper

3/4 cup bread crumbs, soaked in a little milk

Cut mirlitons in half and boil in salted water until tender.

While mirlitons are boiling, in a large skillet

sauté shrimp in butter about 5 minutes; remove from skillet and set aside.

Remove mirlitons from boiling water and drain. When cool, scoop out and mash the pulp, being careful not to damage the outer shell of the mirliton.

In the shrimp skillet, brown onions and garlic in remaining butter; add tomato, parsley, thyme, bay leaf, salt, and pepper. Simmer for a few minutes to blend ingredients.

In a bowl, mix bread crumbs (squeeze out excess milk) with mirliton pulp and salt and pepper to taste. Add this mixture to the vegetables browning in the skillet and fry everything for an additional 5 minutes. Return shrimp to skillet and mix well with vegetables and bread crumbs. Remove from heat.

Use the vegetable-shrimp–bread crumb mixture to stuff the mirliton shells. Place the stuffed mirlitons in a baking dish, dot with butter, and sprinkle with additional bread crumbs. Bake for 15 minutes at 350° until golden brown. Serves six.

GIDGET'S STUFFED SHRIMP MIRLITONS

4 large mirlitons

2 tablespoons butter

1 large onion, chopped

1/2 large bell pepper, chopped

1 stalk celery, chopped

2 cloves garlic, minced

1 pound shrimp, deveined and peeled

1 cup crushed saltine crackers

1 bay leaf

2 tablespoons parsley

Salt and pepper

1 1/2 cups Italian bread crumbs

Parmesan cheese for topping

Cut mirlitons in half lengthwise. Cover with water and bring to a boil. Reduce heat and cook slowly for 20 minutes or until tender. Remove from heat and cool slightly. Scoop out pulp with spoon, leaving a firm shell about 1/4 inch thick. Mash pulp and set aside.

Heat butter in large saucepan. Add onion, bell pepper, and celery and sauté until lightly browned. Add garlic and shrimp; cook shrimp until they turn pink. Add mashed pulp, crackers, bay leaf, parsley, salt, and pepper. Cook on low heat until thoroughly blended. Put mixture into shell. Sprinkle with Italian bread crumbs and Parmesan cheese. Dot with butter. Bake at 350° for 15 minutes, or until lightly browned.

RUTTER BEGGERS (TURNIP HEARTS)

1 pound turnip hearts

1/2 pound bacon

2 smoked ham hocks

3 tablespoons sugar

Peel turnip hearts and cut into wedges. In a skillet, fry bacon. Add turnip hearts, ham hocks, and sugar. Add enough water to cover ingredients. Cook until tender.

NANA'S RICE DRESSING

1/2 pound chicken giblets

1/2 pound chicken livers

1/2 pound pork, chopped

1/2 pound ground beef

Oil to cover bottom of skillet

1 large onion, chopped

1 cup chopped celery

2 cloves garlic, minced

1 bell pepper, chopped

3 cups water

2 (7-ounce) cans mushrooms

1 1/2 cups uncooked rice

Salt and pepper

In a food processor or sausage grinder, grind giblets, livers, pork, and beef. In a skillet, fry in oil until partially cooked. Add onion, celery, garlic, and bell pepper. Cook slowly for 1 hour. Add water, mushrooms, rice, and salt and pepper to taste. Cook slowly in covered pot until rice is done, about 20 minutes.

❦ C.J. ❦

Years back, an Englishman named C.J. lived deep in the swamp in a quaint little houseboat where he had retired to a private life. Occasionally, C.J. suffered fits, thinking he was General Lee going to save the south.

On one particular morning, however, C.J. was quite tranquil 'til a bunch of officers of the law decorated his houseboat like Bonnie and Clyde's car. It all started earlier that day when a couple of fish thieves got caught robbing C.J.'s limb lines. C.J. had shot his shotgun into the sky and told them to leave his limb lines alone. So the fish thieves went to town and fetched the Sheriff and claimed C.J. was trying to kill them. That piece of ridiculous information gave those city boys a chance to have some fun in the swamp.

Luckily Old C.J. took cover behind his cast iron stove, where he was boiling eggs to make The South Will Rise Again Deviled Eggs.

C.J. managed to live—only a few bullet holes—and the officers brought him into custody. While bleeding all over the chair of scrutiny, C.J. said, "Boys, I am from England and I grew up shooting chi-chi birds with one shot from the age of seven. If I wanted to really shoot them boys, I would have."

Poor old C.J. was put away in the crazy house for a few months after his bullet wounds healed. I heard that he was released a much calmer person and never returned to that part of the swamp again. Perhaps while flying over the coo-coo nest, he found a safer one to hide out in.

THE SOUTH WILL RISE AGAIN DEVILED EGGS

6 hard-boiled eggs, halved lengthwise, with yolks removed and reserved for filling

1 teaspoon sweet relish

1 teaspoon chopped green olives

1 teaspoon minced celery

1 tablespoon mayonnaise

1 teaspoon ground horseradish

1/2 teaspoon salt

1/2 teaspoon pepper

Dash lemon juice

Dash Crystal Hot Sauce

Paprika for garnish

In a bowl, mash hard-boiled yolks with all ingredients except halved egg whites and paprika. Mix well, then stuff mixture back into halved egg whites. Garnish with paprika.

CHEDDAR CHEESE GRITS

1 cup quick grits

2 tablespoons butter

1/2 pound grated cheddar cheese

1 egg, beaten

1 teaspoon salt

1/2 teaspoon pepper

In a saucepan, cook grits according to directions on box. Stir in butter and cheese. Add egg, salt, and pepper. Pour mixture into greased casserole dish and bake at 350° for 30 minutes.

ᚹ ORLEANS ᚹ

Orleans was a little anxious knowing hunting season was about to open. He had planned to take off for a vacation to his houseboat in the swamp. He stepped outside his city house with his best friend Earl to check out his hunting rifle. He didn't think he was hurting nothing by firing a few rounds at the vacant lot across the street—long as he wasn't shooting in his neighbor's direction.

After he was satisfied that his rifle was in good working order, he and Earl went back inside to watch the weekend weather. A little while later, a SWAT team arrived outside his house and demanded that he come out with his hands up.

Orleans got so durn mad about living in the city and not being able to shoot his rifle outside his own house that he told the SWAT team that him and Earl were not coming out, and they should mind their own business.

The SWAT team leader decided that Orleans had Earl as his hostage, and told Orleans to remain calm, not to harm Earl. Orleans got even more annoyed for the very thought of them city boys suggesting that he would harm his best friend. So he gave them a showdown to put them in their place.

Orleans said, "Earl is staying in here with me, and y'all can kiss my rear end!"

The SWAT team leader set his men in place, ready to take out Orleans with one shot when they got word. When Orleans finally had his thrill of giving the city boys something to talk about for a long time, he said, "All right, I'm gonna release my hostage, so don't shoot him!" He opened the front door and sent out Earl, who barked at the SWAT team.

"That's a durn dog!" The SWAT team leader blurted out.

"Yep, sure is," Orleans replied.

Orleans had to go in for some evaluation, but they didn't keep him long and he eventually got to go vacation at his houseboat in the swamp where he was able to fire his rifle as much as he wanted to.

TURTLE SAUCE PICANTÉ

1/2 cup flour

1 cup cooking oil

1 large onion, chopped

2 cloves garlic, chopped

1 bell pepper, chopped

1 (14-ounce) can tomatoes

1 (14-ounce) can tomato sauce

3 cups water

1 pound turtle meat

Salt and pepper

1/2 cup chopped green onions

1/2 cup sherry

In a large saucepan or deep skillet, make a roux with flour and oil and cook until medium brown. Add onions and cook until tender. Add garlic, bell peppers, tomatoes, tomato sauce, and water. Cook over low heat for 30 minutes. Add turtle meat, salt, pepper, and green onions. Cook about 45 minutes or until meat is tender. Just before serving, add sherry. Serve over white rice.

🦅 THE HONEY ISLAND SWAMP MONSTER 🦅

A song written by Perry Ford

Way down south, close to New Orleans,
'Bout forty-five miles from town,
Where the swampland meets the hardwoods,
There's a legend going 'round.
Some folks say he's evil,
Cast from a voodoo spell.
He walks upright,
When he screams at night,
You'd swear he came from hell.
Yeah, they call him the Honey Island Monster,
Some say he's just an old wanted man,
Who walks in the shadows of the cypress trees
Way down in Louisian'.
In the swamp there came old trappers,
Tough and rugged old hands,
Claimed they'd seen him many of times
When they hunted and trapped the land.
Late at night by a dim fire light,
You people best beware,
He's standing in the shadows,
Lurking around out there.
They call him the Honey Island Monster,
Believe in him if you can,
'Cause if you spend one night
When the moon is right,
I swear you'll understand.
He walks in the shadows
Of the cypress trees,
Way down in Louisian'.

OLD MAN CHESTER'S MOONSHINE MUNCHIES

1 cup moonshine (you can substitute bourbon)

3 cups brown sugar

1 cup white sugar

1/2 cup sweetened condensed milk

1/4 cup butter

1 cup pecans

1 tablespoon vanilla extract

In a heavy saucepan, mix all ingredients together and cook over medium heat. To test consistency of candy, drop a tiny bit into a cup of cold water. When it forms a soft ball, it is time to remove from heat. Drop spoon-sized balls onto a greased baking sheet. Let cool and serve.

UNCLE DALE'S
RICE PUDDING

6 eggs, beaten

1 cup cooked and chilled white rice

1 cup sugar

1 cup milk

1/2 cup brown sugar

1 cup raisins

1 teaspoon vanilla extract

1 tablespoon freshly ground nutmeg

In a large bowl, mix all ingredients together except for 1 teaspoon of nutmeg, which should be reserved for a garnish. Pour mixture into a 9-by-9-inch buttered baking dish. Sprinkle remaining nutmeg on top. Bake at 375° for 30 minutes.

UNCLE DALE'S
SWEET POTATO ROLLS

6 sweet potatoes

3 eggs

1 (8-ounce) can condensed milk

1 cup sugar

Flour

Butter

Large marshmallows

In a saucepan, cover sweet potatoes with water and boil until soft. Purée in blender or by hand until creamy and smooth. Add eggs, condensed milk, and sugar. Stir well. Add a bit of flour to mixture to stiffen. The mixture should be the consistency of cookie dough.

Spoon out a small portion of mixture onto waxed paper and press into a patty about 1/2 inch thick. Place the patty in a skillet in which you have melted a little butter. Brown lightly on both sides and remove from skillet. Place a marshmallow in the center of each patty. Fold over and seal edges. Place on greased baking sheet. Bake at 300° for 10 to 15 minutes, or until browned.

GRANDMA EMILY'S
TEA CAKES

1 1/2 cups sugar

1 cup solid vegetable shortening

2 1/2 cups self-rising flour

2 tablespoons freshly ground nutmeg

In a mixing bowl, cream sugar and shortening together. Add flour and nutmeg. Mix until the dough doesn't stick to your hand.

Flour a board and roll the dough out to 1/2 inch thick. Cut out individual cakes with cookie cutter or knife and place on a greased cookie sheet. Bake at 375° for 25 minutes or until done.

BRIAN'S HUCKLEBERRY COBBLER

1 1/2 cups flour

1 tablespoon baking powder

3/4 cup buttermilk

1 tablespoon plus 1/4 cup sugar

1 cup huckleberries

In a bowl, using either a spoon or an electric mixer, beat together flour, baking powder, buttermilk, and 1 tablespoon sugar. Turn mixture out onto waxed paper and roll or press to 1/2 inch thick.

Preheat oven to 375°. In a saucepan, combine huckleberries and the 1/4 cup sugar. Bring to a boil, stirring constantly. Pour hot huckleberries into a greased 9-by-13-inch baking pan. Place flattened dough on top. Bake for 35 minutes or until dough rises and becomes browned.

BLACKBERRY DUMPLINGS

4 tablespoons butter, melted, at room temperature

1 cup milk

2 eggs

3 1/2 cups sugar

2 teaspoons vanilla extract

3 1/2 cups flour

3 teaspoons baking powder

4 cups water

1 1/2 quarts blackberries

In a mixing bowl, combine melted butter, milk, eggs, 1 cup sugar, and vanilla.

In a separate bowl, combine flour and baking powder. Add dry ingredients to liquid and stir. Do not overmix.

In a large skillet, combine water, 2 1/2 cups sugar, and blackberries. Cook over medium heat until mixture thickens.

Drop dumpling batter by the spoonful into

blackberry mixture and cook until dumplings rise. Test with fork. When fork comes out clean, remove dumplings and continue adding batter until it is used up. Serve dumplings warm, topped with blackberry mixture.

CHAPTER 6

THE LOWDOWN ON GATOR AND LOUANN: GET-TOGETHER FOODS

THE LOWDOWN ON GATOR AND LOUANN

Six months had gone by since Gator had been released from prison and five months since LouAnn quit waitressing at the Chicken Poop Lounge. Everything seemed to be going pretty smoothly, except that LouAnn had put most of her weight back on. According to her sister, Chantell, who travels the world, she does nothing but cook, eat, and sit around the house watching soap operas while she folds clothes. It suddenly occurred to LouAnn that she was bored to tears with herself and she needed a change.

The phone rang. It was Roxy. "Hun, what are you gonna cook for the Annual Squirrel Hunt Festivity?"

"It's that time again, huh?" LouAnn asked as she folded Gator's long-johns.

Roxy said, "I'm fixin' Alligator Gumbo this year."

LouAnn fantasized, "I think I'll bring red wine and brie."

"What is brie?" Roxy was caught completely off guard.

"Fancy cheese," LouAnn answered without one hint of a joke.

"LouAnn, have you been talking to your sister in Paris again?"

"Not lately," LouAnn told her as she pulled out another load of hot clothes from the dryer.

"I don't think them squirrel hunters are gonna appreciate fancy cheese. And you know the only wine they're gonna be drinkin' at the squirrel hunt party is homemade Muskydine wine," Roxy reminded her.

LouAnn sat in the chair, which, against Gator's approval, is still covered with the pink girly material that her sister sent her from Rome. "I was just kiddin'. I don't know what I'm gonna fix this year." While Roxy chatted on about her Alligator Gumbo dish, LouAnn suddenly remembered a more important detail. "Oh my gosh, that weekend is Gator's birthday, too."

"It sure is, ain't it. You can bake him a cake shaped like a squirrel," Roxy suggested.

"That's a good idea!" LouAnn had come back to the real world. Especially when Roxy added, "Anything but Whiskey Cake." That comment, which was supposed to be funny, only made LouAnn remember why Gator went to jail the last time. She knew she had better stop daydreaming about fancy cheese and red wine.

When LouAnn hung up the phone, she had a new thought. She wanted to lose a few pounds and buy sexy lingerie, since Gator had spent his last birthday with Brutus, his cellmate in prison. First thing was first. LouAnn made a hair appointment with Mona, even though Mona told her she didn't need an appointment because she's like family. LouAnn put the clothes away and went down the road to Mona's Beauty Boutique, which is a salon that Mona's ex-husband had built on her back porch.

"You want a perm?" Mona asked while she made a pot of coffee.

LouAnn replied, "No. I want to go back blond."

Mona stopped in her tracks and turned to LouAnn and asked if she was sure, since Gator had made her color her hair back to its natural shade of brown when he got out of the pen.

LouAnn thought a moment, then answered, "Mix up that same color you used before and just make me some nice highlights."

A half-hour later, Mona could sense that LouAnn was about to be depressed after she took a good long look in the mirror with the plastic cap on her head.

"I can't fit into that cute little outfit I bought at the church garage sale. It woulda been perfect for the Squirrel Hunt Festivity," LouAnn moaned.

Then Mona said, "We can buy some camouflage material and make us a new outfit to match the hunters."

That didn't satisfy LouAnn. She continued, "It ain't just that. I'm tired of sitting in the house all day. I'm gonna lose my mind if I don't get out and do something fun."

Mona suggested that LouAnn join the new gym that opened in town. They could meet there and gossip and take a sauna. LouAnn cheered up until Mona rinsed her hair and spun the chair around toward the mirror. She burst into tears when she got a look at her bright orange highlights. Mona had mixed the wrong concoction. She never was any good at color jobs and her beauty school teacher wasn't there anymore to repair things.

"I can fix it," Mona assured her.

LouAnn wasn't about to go out in the neighborhood with orange highlights, so she bravely let Mona try another color that had a little extra bleach. After two shades of orange and one shade of green, LouAnn and Mona were satisfied with what they finally came up with, but it wasn't just highlights anymore.

"You think Gator's gonna be mad at you?" Mona asked.

"No, he's gonna be mad at you," LouAnn said.

"Tell him it's easier to go darker."

LouAnn was tired of sitting for four hours. "I got to go. I have to make supper for my boys."

"Here. Put this on your head and surprise them," Mona told LouAnn as she covered her head with a scarf.

The truth was that Mona didn't want any potential customers seeing what kind of damage she had done to her friend's hair.

Before LouAnn headed home with the scarf on her head, Mona reminded her about the gym. She could go as a guest with her that night and see if she liked it, since it was Friday and Gator was probably going to the river camp.

When LouAnn got home, no one was there. She fried pork chops and some eggplants that her Mama had given her from the garden. She made a few phone calls around the 'hood looking for her kids. Roxy informed her that they were out in the pirogue. She also informed her that Gator was in the yard helping Scooter get the boat hitched to the truck.

"That figures," LouAnn said, then continued, "Tell Dusty and Ollie I got supper on the table and to hurry up and come eat 'cause I'm gonna go to the gym with Mona later."

"The gym!" Roxy spit out, wanting to hear it all until she noticed that the cornbread was about to burn, so she had to get off the phone.

"Will you watch my boys later tonight?" LouAnn asked before Roxy hung up.

"Sure, but call me when you get back. I want to hear all

about it," Roxy told LouAnn, expecting extraordinary news.

LouAnn loved the gym just like Mona promised her. There were a bunch of exercise machines that she had no idea how to use, but knew she could figure out eventually. And there was a Jacuzzi and steam room and a dry sauna. Mona didn't have to convince LouAnn anymore. The gym was going to be her safe haven. But, convincing Gator to let her join wasn't going to be a picnic—especially since the dues cost almost fifty bucks a month. But, since when does she do everything that Gator wants her to, especially now that she's blond again? She was joining one way or another, even if she had to go back to work at the Chicken Poop Lounge.

Saturday morning, Gator came off the river for a shower. He knew something was fishy when he saw his favorite homemade buttermilk biscuits and gravy on the table waiting for him. He skeptically sat down to eat. That's when LouAnn pitched her idea about the gym. She didn't get through to him until she mentioned waitressing again to pay for it. That was out of the question.

Gator said, "No woman of mine is gonna be working at the Chicken Poop Lounge again." He didn't realize how serious LouAnn was until she took off Mona's scarf. Gator took a second look at the almost yellow blond hair and knew she meant business. "What have you went and done to your hair, woman?"

"Mona did it."

"Tell Mona to find a new line of work," Gator said as he sopped his biscuits in the gravy.

"Well, I like it and I hope it grows on you because it's stayin' this color."

"Yeah, until it falls out," Gator added sarcastically.

LouAnn stared hard for a moment trying to be mad at Gator, but deep down she knew her new hair color was plain awful. She suddenly cracked up laughing. Gator giggled with her until she burst into a fit of tears.

"Now what?" he asked.

LouAnn whaled on about all kinds of things: How bored she was. How fat she was. How poor she was. How many kids she had to clean up after. How many weekends she spent alone because he's always at the camp. How nice her sister has it because she's married to a millionaire. How much she needs to work out at the gym.

Gator reckoned that spurt of ridiculous emotion was one of those woman things. He didn't rightly understand why she suddenly wanted to work out. He was satisfied with her weight. LouAnn told him that she liked herself better when she was clocking the scales at one-forty and she accused him of wanting to keep her fat so nobody else would look at her the way they did when she was wearing size nine. Then she informed Gator that if he can go off to the river camp every weekend and go hunting, just because, then she could go to the gym. But Gator still wasn't convinced. "You give me a better excuse than that."

LouAnn pointed out that she'd probably be in a much better mood when he came off the river on Sunday nights because she'd be relieving stress at the gym. Gator thought a moment of what life would be like with a stress-free wife. He got up from the table and went over to where she was and gave her a kiss on the top of her yellow head. Then he planted the fifty bucks in her hand. "Here's the fifty bucks. But don't you come home skin and bones like last time." LouAnn managed to smile until he said, "I'm going back to the river. I might be home later tonight, but please do somethin' about that yellow hair." Gator made a fast getaway.

LouAnn cried all the way to Wal-Mart, where she picked up a box of hair color in a shade of dark brown.

Later that night, while the men gathered at the river camp to shoot bull and fry fish, Gator told everybody what had occurred. Scooter claimed that LouAnn must be going through the change of life.

"But she's only thirty-eight," Gator argued.

"Some women change sooner than others. Look what Big Bertha did when she turned thirty-six."

"That wasn't a change of life. That was a change of common sense. Any woman who would bug her old man's boat so she could hear what he's talkin' 'bout while he's fishing is completely off her rocker," Darrel commented.

"I was glad when that boat sunk," Earl claimed.

The men had a few more beers while talking about the problems their women cause them.

Then Bubba changed the conversation and said, "Who's killing the hog this year for the Squirrel Hunt?"

It's a ritual every year for someone new to kill a hog. Scooter will smoke the hog on the grill during the event. The men decided that Bubba will have the honor, since he had never shot anything except possums in Mrs. Betty's Chicken Coop.

The Annual Squirrel Hunt Festivity started like it always had the previous years. Saturday morning, the hunters who didn't have a bad hangover went out into the swamp at daybreak and shot a few squirrels. The wives and kids and girlfriends showed up about noon to see who won. But LouAnn hadn't showed up.

"She better get her butt up here," is what Gator was thinking. He asked around for a mobile phone so he could track her down. No luck. Gator had another beer to settle his nerves, but he got to thinking about the fancy New Orleans lawyer who almost stole his old lady right out from under him while he was serving time. He wondered if LouAnn had found herself another business-man to liven up her life, since she claimed to be bored to tears last time they had an argument.

Gator had no idea that LouAnn and Roxy and Mona were waiting up at the boat landing with huge containers of potato salad and pork 'n' beans and Alligator Gumbo and the squirrel-shaped birthday cake that LouAnn was going to surprise him with.

It just so happened to be the exact time that the newspaper reporter and photographer showed up to catch a ride. They had heard about this event last year and didn't want to miss out on a good story this year. The women recognized the camera bag and notepad. "Are y'all from the newspaper?" LouAnn asked with a big natural smile. The gentlemen introduced themselves and com-mented how much they liked the ladies' camouflage outfits. "We made 'em just for the Squirrel Hunt Festivity," LouAnn admitted. The ladies were pleased as pie to see their names get jotted down on the notepad and even more pleased when the men asked if they could take their picture. The women sucked in their bellies and poked out their chests, like they had done for the high school prom pictures.

"That's an interesting squirrel-shaped cake," the reporter commented.

"It's my husband's birthday cake."

The reporter jotted that down too. "What's his name?"

"Gator."

"Is that his real name?" the reporter had to know.

"Are you gonna print it in the paper?"

"If that's all right," the reporter said.

"He'd love to have his name in the paper for somethin' besides being in jail," LouAnn accidentally said.

That was just the icing on the cake. The newspaper people had no idea what they were about to get themselves into.

"Here's our ride!" Roxy said.

The photographer and reporter looked at the Pearl River Queen coming up the waterway. It was a big wooden boat with a tarp than resembled the African Queen, except this one had a rebel flag flying.

"I don't like the idea of being somewhere that we can't make a quick getaway by car if we had to," the photographer said to the reporter as he snapped a picture of Darnell easing the boat to land.

"Pretend we're on a National Geographic adventure," the reporter said. They all climbed into the big boat. It would have normally been a short ten-minute ride up the river to the camp, but the old Pearl River Queen moved at a slower pace.

Fifty boats were already docked by the camp. The band was about to wind up. Gator saw LouAnn in the midst of two business-men and it didn't sit too well with him. Scooter saw the look in Gator's eyes, so he tried to distract him. "Gator, how 'bout stirrin' the squirrel stew."

"Stir it your own self. I got a matter to deal with at the moment," Gator said as he approached his woman, who he knew was flirting with the strangers. "Where the heck you been, LouAnn?" Gator yelled before she could get out of the boat.

"Gator, Hun, these nice people here are the newspaper peo-ple. They want to interview you."

"What for?" Gator asked defensively.

"About how many squirrels you shot on your birthday,

139

silly," LouAnn quickly spurted out.

Gator saw the squirrel cake in her hands and came to his senses.

"I almost forgot about my birthday with all this excitement."

"Your wife is quite determined to get your name in the paper," the reporter said as he cautiously got out of the boat and saw it necessary to show Gator some undivided attention for a few minutes.

Gator eyed him suspiciously, wondering just how determined she was.

"Can we take your picture by your cake, with a few squirrels, sir?" the photographer asked, disrupting his thought.

"Call me Gator. And the squirrels are already in the pot, but here's some squirrel tails." Gator grabbed a handful of squirrel tails and held them up close and didn't even smile until after the picture was taken. Gator would rather be photographed on the more serious side, especially in a hunting interview.

LouAnn followed Roxy and Mona to the picnic table to set out the squirrel cake so everyone could see what a good job she had done.

"Where did you find a squirrel mold?" one lady asked.

"I didn't. I shaped it myself," LouAnn proudly admitted.

"Maybe I'll try to do a deer head for my husband's birthday," the lady said.

LouAnn scanned the crowd to see who was there. She was hoping someone would comment about her weight loss, although it was only ten pounds.

"I hope Gator don't start drinking hard stuff," Roxy told Mona as she uncovered the potato salad.

LouAnn overheard. "He knows better," she assured them.

But what she didn't know was that Gator was about to be offered a swig from Old Man Chester's moonshine jug. "Here's to your birthday, Gator."

"Nah. I better pass on that," Gator said.

"Come on. Be a man." Old Man Chester didn't realize the impact that last statement would have on Gator.

"I'll show you a man," Gator said as he snatched the jug away from Old Man Chester and took a swig.

His friends who knew about his last drinking incident fell silent. Gator was proud of himself for only taking one swig. "That's all I need."

"Take one more to grow on," Old Man Chester dared him.

That's about when Scooter stepped between them and said, "Gator, how 'bout giving me a hand over here?"

Gator knew that Scooter was attempting to prevent a disaster.

"All right, my friend," Gator said as he followed Scooter to the hog pit.

LouAnn took the opportunity to attack Old Man Chester. "You old fool, don't you be givin' Gator no more moonshine. Do you wanna see him go back to prison?"

Chester suddenly realized what a horrible mistake he had made, but he was too drunk to think about it too long. He just apologized and staggered to a nearby chair and sat down and passed out.

The reporter and photographer made their rounds and gathered some very unique information that could make a good story for the outside world, who didn't even know this kind of event occurred just minutes from town.

"I think we should get a boat ride back to civilization before nightfall," the photographer told the reporter.

"You're right. Let me go ask that LouAnn woman," the reporter said, not realizing she was the last person he should go and try to fetch information from.

"M'am, could you help us find a ride out of here?" the reporter asked LouAnn as she was putting candles on the cake.

"Wait for us to sing Happy Birthday to Gator. Don't you want a picture of him blowing out his candles?" LouAnn asked innocently.

"Uh, I guess we can wait for that," the reporter told her.

Gator was watching the conversation from a distance. "That there reporter has been a little too chummy with my old lady."

"Gator, I don't want no trouble up here," Scooter warned him.

Gator ignored Scooter's wish and marched over to LouAnn and the chummy reporter. "I think I've about had enough of you two chit-chattin' like you're old friends."

"Now, Gator, don't go acting like that on your birthday," LouAnn begged.

"Are you planning a new affair with this businessman? Maybe he can fly you to Paris to be with your sister," Gator said without really wanting to. The moonshine had taken over.

"Look, mister. I'm just here for a story," the reporter said.

"I'll give you a story all right," Gator said.

The photographer got a good picture of Gator punching the reporter in the mouth, and a better picture of LouAnn smashing the squirrel cake in Gator's face. And an even better picture of Gator throwing LouAnn into the river. The best shot of all was when Scooter wrestled Gator to the sand. Gator cracked up laughing. "All right. I'm done."

As Earl was easing his boat to the bank, the reporter hopped in. "Please take us to the landing fast," the reporter demanded. The photographer hopped in with them.

Earl didn't ask any questions. He just got them out of there as quick as he could.

"This is the best story we've covered all year," the photographer said as he rewound his film.

"Yeah, but the paper is going to have to pay me more money to risk my life like that," the reporter said as he wiped blood from his busted lip.

At the camp, everything had settled down, but not for long. The band got some people dancing. Gator sat in a chair and didn't move until he sobered up. Louann had found somebody's camouflage hunting jumpsuit to slip into while her clothes dried. Her new figure for sure would not be noticed in that getup. But it was just as well. Gator didn't need any more reasons to get excited. She promised herself to fuss at Old Man Chester for bringing moonshine to the Squirrel Hunt Festivity.

Around ten thirty that night, just about everybody was kicking their heels up on the dance floor.

LouAnn went over to Gator and sat on his lap.

"Did your cake taste good?" she asked.

"It was the best damn squirrel cake I've ever had," Gator said.

They both giggled and made their way to the dance floor. "Baby Doll, did you lose weight?" Gator asked as they did the two-step.

LouAnn was thrilled that he had noticed and she decided that Paris wouldn't be the right place for her even if her sister ever did send for her. Perhaps a short visit one day wouldn't hurt none. But for now, she knew life was good on the river.

GIDGET'S YUMMY POTATOES

8 potatoes

1 (14-ounce) can cream of chicken soup

1 cup sour cream

1/4 cup butter, melted

2 tablespoons onions, chopped

1 1/2 cups grated cheddar cheese

Boil unpeeled potatoes until soft enough to slip skins. Drain, cool, and use a fork to coarsely crumble the potatoes. Spread in a 9-by-13-inch buttered baking dish.

Prepare sauce by mixing together cream of chicken soup, sour cream, butter, and onion. Pour over potatoes. Sprinkle cheese over potatoes and sauce mixture. Bake at 350° for 30 minutes.

SQUIRREL SAUCE PICANTE

2 squirrels, cut up

Salt and pepper

Cayenne pepper

Shortening or vegetable oil for frying

2 onions, chopped

1 clove garlic, chopped

1/2 cup chopped bell peppers

1 tablespoon flour

1/2 cup tomato sauce

Rub squirrels with salt, pepper, and cayenne.

Fill the bottom of a heavy baking pan or large skillet with 1/4 inch of shortening or oil. Add the squirrel meat and brown it on all sides. Remove the meat and reduce the heat to medium; sauté onions, garlic, bell peppers, and flour in the same pan until brown.

Return squirrel meat to pan. Add tomato sauce and enough water to cover meat. Cover with a tight-fitting lid. Simmer for 1 1/2 hours or until squirrel meat is tender. Serve over rice.

SHRIMP CASSEROLE

1 pound shrimp, peeled

1 (3-ounce) bag crab boil

1 1/2 teaspoons salt

2 cups chopped celery

1/2 cup sliced canned chestnuts

2 tablespoons grated onions

2 hard-boiled eggs, chopped

3/4 cup mayonnaise

2 tablespoons freshly squeezed lemon juice

1 cup crushed potato chips

1/2 cup grated cheese

Boil shrimp in water with bag of crab boil and 1 teaspoon salt for 5 minutes. Remove from heat and let steep for 20 minutes. Cool and peel. In a large bowl, mix shrimp, celery, chestnuts, onions, and eggs. In a separate bowl, mix mayonnaise, lemon juice, and 1/2 teaspoon salt. Stir into shrimp-egg mixture. Pour into baking dish and top with potato chips and cheese. Bake at 400° for 25 minutes.

UNCLE PERRY'S BURGER REPTILIOUS

2 pounds ground beef

1 cup bread crumbs

2 eggs

1 teaspoon salt

1 teaspoon pepper

Vegetable oil for frying

1/2 cup flour

2 cups water

1 package brown gravy mix

2 cloves garlic, chopped

1/4 cup chopped onions

In a bowl, mix meat, bread crumbs, eggs, salt, and pepper. Form into a giant hamburger patty. Fry it in a large skillet until brown on both sides.

While meat is browning, make a gravy-roux in a separate pot. To the flour and water, add gravy mix, garlic, and onions. Stir on medium high heat until roux is dark brown.

Pour gravy-roux over meat patty. Cover and cook on medium-low heat for 2 hours to enhance the flavor of the gravy. Serve with bread or rice.

SHRIMP SPREAD

1 cup shrimp

1 bag crab boil

1 (8-ounce) package cream cheese, softened

1/2 cup mayonnaise

1 tablespoon grated onion

1/4 cup prepared French dressing

1 tablespoon Worcestershire sauce

1/2 teaspoon hot pepper sauce

1 bunch green onions, finely chopped

In a deep saucepan, boil shrimp in salted water seasoned with crab boil for 5 minutes. Remove from heat and let the shrimp steep for 20 minutes. Drain, peel, clean, and chop finely. Mix shrimp together with all remaining ingredients. Serve chilled or warm with crackers.

OYSTER PARTY PIE

3 tablespoons butter

3 tablespoons flour

1/4 cup chopped green onions

1/2 cup chopped parsley

1 stalk celery, chopped

3 dozen raw oysters, canned or fresh
(reserve the juice)

1 1/2 cups milk

1 teaspoon salt

1/4 teaspoon pepper

1/2 teaspoon Tony Chachere's Creole Seasoning

1 (9-inch) pie shell, unbaked

Melt butter in a heavy skillet. Add flour and cook over medium heat until light cream-colored. Add green onions, parsley, celery, and oysters. Stir until oysters curl. Add oyster juice, milk, and seasonings. Cook 25 minutes, or until thick. Pour mixture into pie shell and bake at 400° for 30 minutes, or until crust is done.

OYSTER DIP

3 tablespoons horseradish

1/2 cup ketchup

1/2 teaspoon Crystal Hot Sauce

Stir all ingredients together.

This is a delicious dipping sauce for raw oysters. It's safe to keep the fresh dip in the refrigerator, but once raw oysters have been dipped in it, discard the used dip.

MUSKYDINE WINE

1 gallon of muskydine (muscadine) grapes,
crushed to yield 1 gallon of juice

4 gallons water

1 ounce bread yeast

20 pounds sugar

EQUIPMENT

5-gallon fermentation jar or barrel

Cap or lid for fermentation jar, with a 1/4-inch hole
drilled into it to accept clear plastic tubing

2 feet of 1/4-inch clear plastic tubing

Water-filled 1-liter soda bottle

Empty bottles or jars for storing finished wine

Corks or lids for bottles and jars

In a tub or large bucket, mash the muskydine
grapes to extract their juice. Pour the juice into
the 5-gallon fermentation jar and add 4 gallons of
water. Dissolve yeast in an additional 1/2 cup of
warm water, then stir into the grape juice and

water mixture. Add sugar, stirring well to dissolve it.

Seal the fermentation jar with its cap or lid. Thread the 1/4-inch tubing into the hole in the lid, but do not let the tubing touch the juice inside the fermentation container. Run the tubing from the fermentation jar to the water-filled soda bottle, submerging the end in the water. When the juice begins to ferment, it produces lots of gas (carbon dioxide), which must be allowed to escape from the fermentation jar or it will explode. By letting the gas bubble through the plastic tubing and into the water-filled soda bottle, you release the gas from the fermentation jar without allowing any dust or other contaminants into the fermenting wine. (You can achieve the same effect by covering the mouth of the fermentation jar with several thicknesses of clean cheesecloth, held on with a rubber band.)

Set the filled fermentation jar in a dark, warm place (about 75 to 80°). The fermenting juice will foam and bubble for about 2 weeks. When the bubbling stops, the solids will settle to the bottom of the fermentation jar and the wine will be almost clear. You can drink it now, or if you want to increase the alcoholic "kick" of the wine, add another 1/2 ounce of yeast and 10 additional pounds of sugar to the wine and let it ferment, covered, for an additional 2 weeks. When this second fermentation stops and the wine is clear, pour it off carefully into storage bottles or jars, being careful not to stir up the sediment from the bottom of the fermentation jar. Serve chilled.

NOTE: You can use this recipe to make wine with any fruit or berry available.

BIG DADDY'S PORK PIE

2 pounds ground pork

1/2 cup chopped onion

1/2 cup chopped bell pepper

2 cloves garlic, minced

1/3 cup chopped parsley

1 teaspoon salt

1/4 teaspoon marjoram

1/8 teaspoon ground cloves

1/8 teaspoon ground mace

Black pepper

Tony Chachere's Creole Seasoning

2 tablespoons flour

2 beef bouillon cubes

1 cup hot water

2 (9-inch) prepared unbaked pie shells

Sauté pork, onion, bell pepper, and garlic in a
large skillet until pork is browned and vegetables
are soft. Stir in parsley, salt, marjoram, cloves,
mace, pepper, and Tony Chachere's Creole

155

Seasoning. Cover and simmer over low heat for 30 minutes. Drain excess fat from skillet. Blend flour into meat mixture. Dissolve bouillon cubes in hot water. Add to mixture. Return to heat and bring to a boil. Simmer for 1 minute, stirring constantly. Remove from heat and set aside to cool. Pile meat mixture into pie shell. Top with other shell. Seal edges. Bake at 400° for 45 minutes.

SWAMP JULEP

2 ounces dark bourbon whiskey
1 tablespoon warm honey
1 teaspoon crème de menthe liqueur
1 tall glass crushed ice

Mix ingredients, shake well, and pour over tall glass of crushed ice. Drink slowly through a straw if you have one. If not, just sip as usual.

THE REAL SOUTHERN MINT JULEP

2 ounces bourbon

1 tablespoon mint syrup (see recipe this page)

Shaved ice

Mint sprig to garnish

Mix the bourbon and syrup, pour over shaved ice, and serve in a frosted silver cup. Garnish with a sprig of mint.

MINT SYRUP

2 cups chopped mint

1 cup sugar

2 cups water

In a saucepan, crush mint into sugar. Add water and bring to a boil. Stir until sugar is dissolved; remove from heat. Cover and let cool. Strain to remove mint leaves. This makes enough for about 45 drinks. You can store extra mint syrup in a corked bottle for your next party.

INDEX